Sabba[...]
Program Planner

Book Four

Sabbath School Program Planner

Book Four

Dorothy Eaton Watts

14 Creative Programs

REVIEW AND HERALD® PUBLISHING ASSOCIATION
HAGERSTOWN, MD 21740

The author assumes full responsibility for the accuracy of all facts and quotations as cited in this book.

This book was
Edited by Richard W. Coffen
Designed by Bill Kirstein
Cover design by Helcio Deslandes
Typeset:10.5/12.5 Times Roman

PRINTED IN U.S.A.

99 98 97 96 95   5 4 3 2 1

R&H Cataloging Service
Watts, Dorothy (Eaton), 1937—
     Sabbath school program planner/ book 4.

     1. Sabbath schools. 2. Worship programs. 1. Title.

          268.86732

ISBN 0-8280-0893-0

Contents

Interview

Celebrity Hour

1

Preparation

Remove the pulpit. Arrange the platform with two chairs in the center as for a TV talk show. Cardboard boxes turned upside down over easels make excellent TV cameras, and these add to the program. *(Or borrow two video camcorders from members of the congregation.)* Write "SDA TV" on the sides of the boxes. Borrow a couple of primary boys to run the "cameras" for you. They will love it if you have a couple of headphone sets to plug into the cameras as well. Cardboard tubes serve well as lenses.

(It is very effective to have characters come in costume, but it is not mandatory for the success of the program.)

Program

Host: Welcome to *Celebrity Hour!* We are pleased that you are with us today in our studio audience. We have some fascinating people for you to meet. Our first is none other than John Zebedee—fisherman, evangelist, author, apostle, and prophet. *(Enter John.)*

John, we welcome you to *Celebrity Hour.* Please sit down. Tell me, John, are you able to point to any particular incident in your life that you consider the turning point? Is there one golden moment of opportunity that, when grasped, made you the famous person you are today?

John Zebedee: Yes. It would be that day in A.D. 27 when I stood on the bank of the Jordan River and saw John the Baptist point to Jesus of Nazareth and say, "Behold, the Lamb of God!"

I did not fully understand those words, but they thrilled me! Moved by an irresistible impulse, Andrew and I followed Jesus. We were eager to speak with Him, yet awed and silent—lost in the overwhelming significance of the thought *Is this the Messiah?*

Jesus understood our longing and invited us to go home with Him. We stayed all day and talked. My life was never the same again. I had met Jesus Christ, the Son of the living God!

Host: John, because of you, many of us in this room have come to feel the same wonder, beauty, and love that you felt in Jesus' presence. Because of you, millions have come to believe in Him as the Messiah, the Saviour of the world.

I love your descriptions of Jesus in the book of Revelation. I wonder, would you do us the favor of reading a little from one of your books?

John Zebedee: I'm reading from my Gospel, chapter 1, verses 1 through 14.

SCRIPTURE READING

Host: Thank you, John Zebedee, for being with us on *Celebrity Hour!* Our next guest lived in more recent times! *(Enter Ellen G. White.)* Ellen G. White—Adventist pioneer, author, lecturer, and prophet. What a joy to have you with us on *Celebrity Hour!*

Most of us here today are your fans! We have your books and quote you often! Today we would like to explore the beginning of our worldwide mission program as a church. In the very beginning of the Advent movement did you envision a worldwide church work?

Ellen G. White: No. It was our common thought in those early days that if the third angel's message was preached throughout the United States to all the nationalities that had come here to seek a refuge, our task would be done.

Host: Didn't the Lord reveal to you in vision that the message was to go to the whole world?

Ellen G. White: Oh, yes indeed! In my vision at Dorchester, Massachusetts, in November 1848 I was instructed to tell James to start a paper, and from "this small beginning it was shown to me to be like streams of light that went clear around the world."

Host: How did the early Adventists feel about this? Did they accept the concept readily?

Ellen G. White: It was difficult for them. They could not understand how, with their few numbers and small resources and limited time, they could possibly encompass the world.

Our enemies were not slow to taunt us. Said one, "It will take you 144,000 years to do what you propose!" "What!" others scoffed, "three preachers—James White, Mrs. White, and Joseph Bates—with fewer than 100 followers, none of them with a red cent, going out with a few little tracts to conquer the world! Preposterous assumption!"

Host: What really happened to wake up Adventists to the possibility of the task?

Ellen G. White: Some of those who accepted the message in America began to share the message with relatives back in the Old Country. An interest developed, and we began getting calls for help.

In 1871 I wrote: "Missionaries are needed to go to other nations to preach the truth. . . . Every opportunity should be improved to extend the truth to other nations. This will be attended with considerable expense, but expense should in no case hinder the performance of this work" (*Life Sketches*, pp. 205, 206).

Three years later I wrote: "You are entertaining too limited ideas of the work for this time. You are trying to plan the work so you can embrace it in your arms. You must take broader views. Your light must not be put under a bushel or under a bed, but on a candlestick, that it may give light to all that are in the house. Your house is the world" (*ibid.,* pp. 208, 209).

I specifically mentioned Europe, Australia, the islands of the seas—all nations, tongues, and peoples.

Host: If I remember correctly, by the General Conference session in August of 1874 the brethren were beginning to catch your vision of a world work.

Ellen G.White: Yes. At that session they voted to send John Nevins Andrews as our first missionary to Europe. We sent the best man we had to carry the Advent message to Europe.

Host: And that was only the beginning. Today thousands of missionaries work in nearly every country of the globe. In fact, today the majority of our members live outside the United States.

Ellen G. White: This is just as I saw it in my first vision in December 1844. The world was spread out before me, and I saw darkness like a pall of death. What did it mean? I could see no light. Then I looked up and saw a bright light that was guiding people toward a heavenly "city" and its Maker. Those people were the believers in Jesus Christ.

Host: But what concerns me is that our people seem to be losing sight of the world vision. More and more we hear people say, "We need to care for the work at home first." Many Sabbath schools do not have the mission report. Sabbath school offerings are not keeping pace with the needs of the world field. Millions have never heard the name of Christ. It takes money to take the light to them. This is certainly an area in which our Sabbath school needs to improve. Have you any counsel for us?

Ellen G. White: "If God's people had the love of Christ in the heart; if every church member were thoroughly imbued with the spirit of self-denial; if all manifested thorough earnestness, there would be no lack of funds for home and foreign missions; our resources would be multiplied; a thousand doors of usefulness would be opened, and we would be invited to enter. Had the purpose of God been carried out by His people in giving the message of mercy to the world, Christ would have come to the earth, and the saints would ere this have received their welcome into the city of God" (*Selected Messages*, book 1, p. 82).

(The basis of this interview is found in *Origin and History of Seventh-day Adventists*, by Arthur W. Spalding, vol. 2, chap. 10.)

Host: Thank you, Mrs White, for your timely counsel. Our next guest is one of the thousands of Adventist workers in lands outside North America. *(Enter representative from another world division, the person who wrote today's mission report.)* _____, we welcome you to *Celebrity Hour!* Please tell our studio audience where you live and what work you do.

Mission Representative: (Gives the place and assignment from today's mission report.)

Host: It is wonderful that you could be with us today! We have just been discussing the beginnings of SDA missions and the tremendous progress that has been made during the past 120 years. We are interested in knowing about the progress of the work in your area. How many countries are in your division?

Mission Representative: There are _____ countries. They are: *(Lists the countries.)*

Host: The countries of your division have been much in the news of late. Has all of the political unrest kept back the progress of our church? *(Adapt to news in this particular section of the world.)*

Mission Representative: Not at all. *(Gives a brief summary of the number of churches, baptized members, etc., as gleaned from the current mission quarterly.)*

Host: That is marvelous! You must have some thrilling soul-winning stories to share with us. Won't you do that just now?

Mission Representative: Thank you, I'd love to. *(Gives mission report.)*

MISSION REPORT

Host: Thank you, _____, for that thrilling report. Coming onto the platform next is Dr. Isaac Watts—world renowned clergyman, theologian, and hymn writer! Welcome to *Celebrity Hour!* How many hymns have you written?

Dr. Watts: 761.

Host: How many are in our new *SDA Hymnal*? And would you please mention two or three of them?

Dr. Watts: There are 25 in the current hymnal. There were 31 in the old hymnbook. Some you might know are: "Joy to the World," "Marching to Zion," and "When I Survey the Wondrous Cross."

Host: I have read about the day you were standing near a restaurant with some friends and you overheard a man ask, "Who is that odd-looking little man?"

"It is Isaac Watts," someone answered.

"Really? Is that the great Dr. Watts?" the surprised man questioned, startled by your shortness in height.

And what was your reply? I understand you stopped right there and told him what you thought!

Dr. Watts: "Were I so tall to reach the pole,
Or grasp the ocean with my span,
I must be measured by my soul:
The mind's the standard of the man."

Host: I'm sure our studio audience would love the story about how you began writing hymns. Please share that with us briefly.

Dr. Watts: One morning when I was 10 years old I was kneeling with my parents for worship, when I began to giggle. As soon as the prayer was finished, Father asked, "Isaac, why did you laugh during prayers?"

I pointed to the bell rope that hung by the fireplace and said, "I saw a little mouse run up the rope, and these lines came into my head:

"There was a mouse for want of stairs,
Ran up a rope to say his prayers."

Father decided I must have a lesson administered to the seat of my pants! I began to cry and said:

"Oh, Father, Father, pity take,
And I will no more verses make."

Despairing of getting me to stop making verses, Father suggested that I use this ability to create better songs for the church worship services. I accepted that challenge.

Host: We are certainly glad that you did, Dr. Watts. Now, in your honor we would like to sing one of your hymns, No. 103 in *The SDA Hymnal*, "O God, Our Help."

OPENING SONG

Host: Our last guest this morning is Elder James White—editor, author, publisher, builder, administrator, and leader of people. What a privilege it is to have you with us today on the *Celebrity Hour!* Is it true that you attended school for less than one year?

James White: That's right! I was a sickly boy and had weak eyesight. I didn't attend school until I was 19. I went for 12 weeks and qualified for a teaching certificate. Later I attended for 19 weeks. A total of seven months.

Host: Incredible! You must have been a genius to accomplish so much in such a short time! You were one of the first editors of *Adventist Review.* You started *Youth's Instructor.* In fact, isn't it true that you wrote the first Sabbath school lessons?

James White: Yes, that in the summer of 1852, just eight years after the Great Disappointment. Ellen and I were living in Rochester, New York, at the time.

Host: Tell us a little about the circumstances under which you wrote those early Sabbath school lessons.

James White: How well I remember that summer! The plague of cholera was raging in the city. Ellen and I had appointments at various meetings from Rochester to Bangor, Maine. We planned to take a monthlong trip to meet these appointments. Just as we were preparing to leave that August, our youngest child, Edson, came down with cholera. How could we leave?

We had special prayer for him. He recovered, though he remained weak. We placed him on a pillow, climbed into the covered buggy, and drove 20 miles that first day.

Our hosts that night said, "If you go on, you'll bury that child by the roadside." But we had to go on, so we did.

We drove about 50 miles after that, stopping only at lunchtime to let the horse rest and feed. Using my lunch box or the top of my black hat for a table, I composed some of those early lessons.

Host: What were some of the topics you covered in those first lessons?

James White: The Sabbath, the Second Coming, the book of Daniel, and the sanctuary service were the main topics of interest back then.

Host: Elder White, we are thankful that you began the Sabbath school lesson plan. In fact, it's time now for us to have our lesson study. Before we separate, will you please lead us in prayer?

PRAYER

Miniseminars

Spiritual Olympics

2

Preparation

This program is for use during one of the years when either the summer or winter Olympic games are held, which is now every two years. Put up several posters of sports action that suggest the Olympic Games. You will find these with a spiritual message in Christian bookstores.

Program

In the next few weeks the summer/winter Olympic Games in _____ will be much in the news. Scores of athletes from around the world will compete before thousands of spectators. Everyone wants to leave with a gold medal, but only a few will. How *do* you get a gold medal in the Olympic Games or in the game of life? Today we will discover that the process is just the same. We are all running in a marathon for eternity, whether we realize it or not.

SCRIPTURE READING: 1 Corinthians 9:24-27

PRAYER

Leader: So how do you run to receive the prize? How do you win your gold medal for eternity?

Speaker 1: How to Get a Gold Medal

A trolley car rattled down the street of Abo, Finland, with teenager Paavo Nurmi behind it. As the trolley gathered speed, Paavo quickened his pace to match. His wiry legs beat a steady rhythm on the pavement, his body moving with them like a well-oiled machine. His broad chest rose and fell as his lungs tried to keep up with his increased need for oxygen. Beads of sweat stood on his high forehead and moistened his back.

"Hurry, Paavo," a friend called from the sidewalk. "You can catch it!"

"Faster, Paavo, faster," another called.

"Why doesn't the conductor stop?" a stranger asked. "You'd think he'd see how badly the boy needs to get on!"

"Paavo doesn't really want to catch the trolley," his friend explained with a laugh. "Chasing the trolley is his way of training for the Olympics. He does this every day during lunch."

"He must really want to win!" the visitor said. "That'll be the day you'd find me chasing a trolley car down Main Street!"

The visitor was right. Winning was the passion of Paavo Nurmi. Although he had to go to work as a laborer when he was 12, he never gave up his dream. He used every spare moment to run, strengthening his muscles and mastering the skills he needed to win.

When the day came for Paavo to run in the 1924 Olympics, his body was ready. He had mastered the skills of running and came away with three gold medals.

Three main factors led to Paavo Nurmi's gold medals. *(Write them on the chalkboard, or display a chart on which they are already written.)*

1. He *wanted* to be a winner.
2. He *believed* he could be a winner.
3. He *prepared* to be a winner.

Paavo Nurmi prepared to be a winner by organizing his life for skills mastery. He practiced running every day so that he was ready when the big event came.

Speaker 2: Wanting to Win

Let's transfer these rules to our spiritual life. First of all, we must consider whether or not we *want* to win. Do you want a closer walk with God more than anything else in life? Is overcoming temptation an obsession with you? Are you willing to make every other aspect of your life fit into your goal of achieving eternal life?

Jeremiah 29:13 states it like it is: "Ye shall seek me, and find me, when ye shall search for me with all your heart." The psalmist says that he longed for God as a thirsty deer looking for a water hole. Finding God was all that mattered.

The rich young ruler lacked this all-consuming passion to know God and live for Him. He wanted the gold medal as long as it didn't cost him too much. He wanted to win in the game of life, but not with his whole heart.

How much do you want to win the race of life? Enough to give up some of the bad habits that are preventing your victory? How much do you want a personal relationship with Jesus? Enough to spend time every day talking to Him and listening to Him talk to you through His Word?

It takes sacrifice to win a gold medal in the Olympics. It takes no less self-sacrifice to win a crown of life, but I am determined to make that sacrifice. I want to win!

Speaker 3: Believing You Can Win

So you want to win, but do you *believe* you can win? Look at yourself. Do you have what it takes to be saved? Are you so perfect that you can live in the presence of a holy God? Do you meet the requirements for receiving an everlasting crown?

When I look at myself, I do not see how I can be saved. As hard as I try, I cannot, it seems, reach the standard God has set. I am not perfect. My righteousness is like filthy rags. My attempts to win the race leave me far, far behind. No, when I look at myself, my past achievements, and my present abilities, I do not believe I can win.

But then I take my eyes off myself and my attempts to run the race. Instead, I look to Jesus. I know that He has the ability to get a gold medal. He has already won the race. He *knows* how it is done. He did it for me! With Him all things are possible. I can grasp the victory "through Christ which strengtheneth me."

Each morning I will surrender myself to Him. I will follow His guidance. I will do as He directs. I will keep in step with Him. When I fall down, He will help me rise again. I will trust in His keeping, sustaining, impelling power. Together we will win! God promises it, and I believe it! By faith I claim the victory! Through faith the gold medal is mine!

Speaker 4: Preparing to Win

What about you? Do you want to win in life's Olympics? Do you want to be a winner? Of course you do. Deep inside every one of us wants to be a winner. We want to win an everlasting gold medal. We want to be saved.

There you have it! We have met the first requirement for winning. We *want* to win.

Do you *believe* you can win? I believe you can win, because Christ has promised to help you. It *is* possible!

The catch comes with the third requirement for winning: *being prepared.* Are you practicing every day, learning the skills that will help you win a gold medal in the eternal Olympics? What are the skills you and I need to master in order to be a winner in the spiritual Olympics? What skills can you practice daily that will prepare you for the final great competition that is coming?

(Make a list on the chalkboard as they name them. Use a roving mike if your church is large. You should get such answers as: Learning to trust God, learning to pray, learning to wait on God, learning to stand up for what we believe, learning to say no, learning to obey God, learning to live clean lives, learning to listen to God's voice, learning to love others, etc.)

All these things we can do today, tomorrow, and every day. All these things we must do if we want a gold medal.

Our brothers and sisters in _____ want to win as much as you and I. They face the same temptations and struggles. _____ has a report of how Adventist believers in _____ are running the race.

MISSION REPORT

How to Get Yourself Elected

3

Preparation

Each speaker comes in carrying a campaign poster that has his or her name on it ("Mike for President!" "Vote for Beth," "Bob Is a Winner," etc.). On the reverse of the poster is a rule for being a winner, which he or she displays at the appropriate time. To make the presentation more effective, decorate with helium balloons in patriotic colors and wall posters with slogans such as: "Be a Winner!" or "You Can Do It!" or "Reach for the Top!" or "Go for It!"

Creative superintendents might try inserting a musical fanfare as each candidate enters. Try to work up some of the excitement of a political campaign.

Program

The people of _____ (name of country) have had months of campaign speeches and political whoop-de-do that will climax in a few days with the election of a _____. How do people get themselves elected? How do they become winners? How can *you* become a winner? That's the topic of our special feature this morning. To give us some advice we have three presidential hopefuls with us.

Talk 1: Winners Believe in Themselves

Winners win because they look at themselves and see a winner. They believe that they can accomplish anything they want to accomplish. They know they can achieve. They are unwilling to accept someone else's negative evaluation, for they know that God created them to reach the top, to succeed. Winners know that the power to be a winner lies within themselves, nowhere else. They aren't looking for success to come from their connections or from luck. They are looking within themselves and seeing that they have what it takes to succeed. Winners feel responsible for their own destiny.

Losers are always blaming somebody or something else for their failures. "My parents were losers." "My boss doesn't like me." "I wasn't born with enough brains." "Everybody else gets all the breaks." "People are prejudiced against me." "I don't have nice clothes." "I wasn't born on the right side of the tracks."

Once there was a man selling balloons in the streets of New York City. When business was slack, he released a balloon, first one color and then another. Each time a balloon floated upward, a new crowd gathered and he sold several balloons. The balloon man noticed a small African-American boy standing at the edge of the crowd. He was watching the different colored balloons rise toward the sky. At last he came close to the balloon man, looked up into his eyes, and asked, "Mister, if you released a black balloon, would it go up?"

"Of course," the balloon man answered. "It's what's inside the balloons that make them go up!"

So be a winner! It's what's inside you that matters. You have what it takes. You can "do all things through Christ!" With Him "all things are possible!" With His help you can succeed!

(Display sign: "Winners Believe in Themselves.")

Talk 2: Winners Set Goals

Imagine for a moment a Super Bowl game. The players are in their dressing rooms, and the coach is giving a pep talk. "This is it, fellows. It's now or never! We win or lose all tonight. Go out there and give it all you've got!"

The players, charged up, run onto the field and stop short in confusion. There are no goal lines and no goalposts. How can they play without goal lines and goalposts? They wouldn't know which way to run or which direction to kick the ball. There's no way the game could go on. There'd be no winners without goals, and that's just as true in the game of life as it is in a game of football.

Losers don't plan to fail. They just don't plan anything. By not planning to go somewhere, they get nowhere. It's pretty hard to reach a destination you don't have.

Winners have definite, precise, clearly set goals that help them realize their maximum potential. Winners are forever setting goals. Some are little goals that can be accomplished today, some take a week or a month, but all point to their overall main goal in life. There are many kinds of goals we need to set: physical, financial, spiritual, career, family, mental, and social. If you would be a winner, take the time to think about these different areas of your life and set a goal in each one. Write it down somewhere so that it will be clear where you are going. Try making lists of goals and checking them off as you accomplish them. You will find yourself becoming a winner. Once J. C. Penney said, "Give me a stock clerk with a goal, and I will give you a man who will make history. Give me a man without a goal, and I will give you a stock clerk."

(Display sign: "Winners Set Goals.")

Talk 3: Winners Don't Give Up

Believing you can win, setting a goal, and starting out toward that goal are not enough to make you a winner. To be a winner you must reach your goal. Winners want to win badly enough that they keep going despite all odds. They don't give up.

A lot of people with high IQs are leading mediocre lives. Many with great talents achieve very little. Winners are not always the brightest kids in the class or the persons voted most likely to succeed.

Harry was an inner-city boy whose counselor told him he didn't have what it took to go to college—his scores were too low. Harry didn't listen. He wanted to become a doctor, so he went to college. He knew he could do it; it just might take more work and more time. When others spent five hours on a paper, he spent 30, but he got his Ph.D. in health sciences and owns a large chain of health-food stores today. Harry is a winner.

Wilma Rudolf wanted to become an Olympic Gold Medal winner, but she was crippled from polio. In spite of her condition, she was determined to be a world-class athlete. At the age of 20 she became the first woman to win three Olympic gold medals in track and field. With persistence and a lot of hard work, Wilma accomplished what seemed to be impossible.

Thomas Edison said that genius is 1 percent inspiration and 99 percent perspiration.

Winners are hard workers who don't give up. Success is often failure turned inside out. If you want to win badly enough, you will find a way to make it happen.

(Display sign: "Winners Don't Give Up.")

The worldwide network of schools, hospitals, and churches that our denomination operates is a testimony to people who did not give up, regardless of the obstacles thrown in their pathway. They believed they were called of God to spread the church's influence in other lands. They had a vision of what could be accomplished. They set goals. And they kept working until, by God's grace, they accomplished those goals.

There are men and women of the same caliber carrying on the work of the church in mission lands. Today we hear from one of these winners in _____.

MISSION REPORT

Modern Parables

Roadblocks to Friendship

4

Preparation

Arrange three sawhorses, chairs, or a visual aid you can think of to represent a roadblock. Make three signs for road blocks, each containing one word of the following: ROADBLOCKS TO FRIENDSHIP. On the back of the "roadblocks" sign write the word "Judging." On the back of the "to" sign write the words "Sending Solutions." On the back of the "friendship" sign write the words "Avoiding Other's Concerns." Attach the signs so that they can be turned over at the appropriate time.

Write the 50 roadblocking statements on separate cards or slips of paper. Mix them up and divide them among the members present. An alternative would be to have several voices give these over a hidden mike.

Use a different speaker for each barricade.

Program

Imagine for a moment that friendship is a two-way street. I want to enjoy your companionship. You want to be my friend too. We both set out on this road of friendship, hoping to meet, but roadblocks bar the way. We try to communicate, but turn around disappointed. Have you had that frustrating experience? Have you tried to be friends only to face a roadblock?

Lisa had that problem every time she went home for vacation. After her last visit she sighed and said, "Well, I blew it again! I resolved that it would be a pleasant visit. But I wasn't there five minutes before my mother started criticizing the way I wore my hair and the length of my skirt. Dad joined in. I got mad. We argued for half an hour, and I ended up walking out. Mom was in tears, and I was seething. It happens every time I go home. I always end up putting my foot in my mouth and saying the wrong thing. I know I should be more like Jesus, but I don't know how. Nothing seems to work."

What about the conflicts you and I face? How can we communicate better with our children, colleagues, and friends? How can we really get somewhere on the street called Friendship? Obviously we'll have to tear down the barricades that impede our progress. The roadblocks to friendship have got to go! What are the barricades we need to remove?

Today you will all help with the feature. As each speaker describes one of the types of roadblocks, he or she will call for the illustrations from you. You may give the one you have been given or a similar one that you feel would fit the classification called for. They will call for the roadblocks by number.

Barricade 1: Judging

(Turn over the "judging" sign.)

A famous psychiatrist once said that he believed the major barrier to friendship lies in our natural tendency to judge others. We are prone to evaluate the feelings and statements of other people, forgetting that judgmental statements block friendship and communication. We must learn how to accept other people without judging them as good or bad, right or wrong. Let's look at some examples of ways that we judge.

One way we judge is by

Criticizing. Let's hear some examples of criticizing. Roadblocks 1 to 4.

1. You're not thinking straight!
2. That's not the way to do things!
3. What a stupid thing to say!
4. Is that any way for a Christian to talk?

Calling names and *labeling* prevent us from really getting to know a person. When we call names we do not see an individual, but a type. We are lumping people together as though they were all the same. What are some labels we give? Roadblocks 5-11.

    5. Stupid
    6. Brat
    7. Egghead
    8. Jerk
    9. Dummy
   10. Weirdo
   11. Creep

Another effective way we judge is by

Diagnosing. We play emotional detective and then act as though we know exactly what others are thinking and why they do things. Examples are roadblocks 12-16.

   12. You're saying this because you're angry.
   13. You're just jealous!
   14. You just want to look good.
   15. You're a bit paranoid.
   16. What you really need is . . .

Praising evaluatively is sometimes used as a way to get people to change. When we have this purpose in mind, we are trying to manipulate another person. It is a form of judging, and it turns people off. Some examples are roadblocks 17-19.

   17. You usually have good judgment.
   18. You have so much potential!
   19. You are smart enough to know better!

Barricade 2: Sending Solutions.

(Turn over second sign.)

When people are having problems, some of us like to send solutions. Sending solutions creates new problems without solving the old. Sending solutions arouses strong negative feelings in the other person and derails the conversation.

One way we send solutions is by

Ordering and *threatening*. These are solutions backed with force. They produce negative results. Some examples are roadblocks

31

20-25.

    20. You've got to do this.

    21. Stop it!

    22. Go and apologize.

    23. You'd better not try that again!

    24. You'd better do this, or else . . .

    25. I warn you that if . . .

Preaching and *advising* are other more caring forms of sending solutions. When we try to advise others, we are insulting their intelligence by suggesting that they can't handle their own difficulties. Advising shows a lack of confidence in others. Preaching is an indirect form of force because it is trying to use the power of God or social authority to get others to do what we want them to do. Some examples of these manipulative attitudes are roadblocks 26-32.

    26. You should do this.

    27. You ought to try it.

    28. It's your responsibility.

    29. I urge you to do this.

    30. I think you should . . .

    31. It would be best if you . . .

    32. Let me suggest that . . .

Interrogating is a strong barrier to communication. Some questions are necessary, but extensive questions put people on the defensive. Questions can be a way of trying to manipulate. They can make others feel uncomfortable. Examples are roadblocks 33-36.

    33. Why did you do that?

    34. How long have you felt that way?

    35. What have you done about it?

    36. Who influenced you to make that decision?

Barricade 3: Avoiding the Other's Concerns

(Turn over last sign.)

Friendship demands that we care about others and be interested in what concerns them. Some roadblocks show that we really care

32

very little about what is bothering the other person.

Diverting is a way of switching a conversation from the other person's concerns to our own topic. We often try to divert the topic to one that is more comfortable for us. Some examples are road-blocks 37-40.

37. Let's have lunch and forget it.
38. That reminds me of the time that . . .
39. You think you've got problems!
40. Not to change the subject, but . . .

Logical argument is a roadblock that can be infuriating. Logic focuses on facts and avoids feelings. When we use logic to avoid emotional involvement, we are withdrawing from the other person. Logical argument puts distance between people. Some examples are roadblocks 41-44.

41. Do you realize that . . .
42. The facts are in favor of . . .
43. Let me give you the facts.
44. Experience tells us that . . .

Reassurance is a way of seeming to comfort another person while actually doing the opposite. We reassure people when we are feeling uncomfortable with their emotional demands and don't want to get involved. Reassurance stops communication because it is not hearing what the other person is actually expressing. Examples are roadblocks 45-50.

45. You'll feel better tomorrow.
46. Things will get better.
47. It's darkest just before dawn.
48. It's not all *that* bad!
49. Don't worry! Everything will turn out OK.
50. Cheer up! Things could be a lot worse!

Leader: Roadblocks to friendship. Barricades to communication. Let's get rid of them! *(Remove all the barricades as you speak.)*

Free at Last!

5

Preparation

Arrange for one roving mike (more if your church is large). Buy a set of plastic handcuffs at a toy store. Also, buy or borrow 12 to 15 feet of chain. Arrange for a hidden microphone for the skit.

Program

In September 1620 a small band of Pilgrims, led by William Brewster, left Plymouth, England, for the New World. Twelve years before, they had fled persecution in England. After a few years as strangers in that land, they decided to go to America, where they could not only have freedom to worship God but also freedom to raise their children according to their own customs. They preferred farming to city life. Moreover, their children were learning to speak Dutch, and the Pilgrims feared that they would soon be more Dutch than English. America seemed the perfect answer. There they would be free at last!

The Pilgrims picked up a few others in England and sailed for the New World in the *Mayflower*. After weathering 65 days of stormy seas, half the Pilgrims died during that first difficult winter on the wild New England coast.

The term *pilgrim* was a good name for those 102 people who sailed on the *Mayflower*, for the word means "wanderer" or "way-farer." These people were strangers in a strange land, wandering from place to place in search of religious freedom. They were like Abel, Enoch, Noah, Abraham, Isaac, and Jacob—strangers and pil-grims on the earth who longed for a better country where they would be free at last.

Are not you and I pilgrims and strangers in this old world? This is not our permanent home. We are going to a better land where there will be no more pain, sickness, sorrow, or crying. We are going to a better land where we will be free at last! A favorite song of the early Adventist believers was "I'm a Pilgrim," No. 444 in *The SDA Hymnal*. Soon Jesus will come to take us to heaven, where we will be pilgrims no more. Free at last!

OPENING SONG: "I'm a Pilgrim"

PRAYER

"Free at Last" (A Skit)
(Speaker walks onto the platform holding up his hands, which are handcuffed together. A chain is wrapped around the upper portion of his body. The "voice" comes from a hidden mike.)
Speaker: I am an American (Canadian)! I live in the land of the free! I am free!
Voice: Free? You are not free!
Speaker: Oh, but I am!
Voice: Then why the handcuffs? Why the chains?
Speaker: Well, yes . . . But I live in the land of the free; therefore I am free.
Voice: The land may be free, but you are not. You are a slave.
Speaker: Oh, no! Didn't you know that the slaves were freed more than 120 years ago?
Voice: Nevertheless, because of your human condition, you are a slave, and the chains that bind you are many.
Speaker: I think I'm beginning to understand. Tell me more. What are these chains that bind me?
Voice: Death, sorrow, suffering, sickness, handicaps, heartaches, sinful desires, temptations, weakness, fear, crime, loneliness, pain, poverty, hunger, insecurity, hatred, war, bigotry, prejudice, persecution. These you cannot escape, for you were born on Planet Earth.
Speaker: But must I always be like this? Is there no hope?
Voice: Ah, yes! There is hope! Jesus is coming soon! He holds the key to your handcuffs! He will remove your chains! Then, set

36

free from earth's gravity, you will travel with Him to the heavenly home He has prepared for you. "And God shall wipe away all tears from [your] eyes; and there shall be no more death, neither sorrow, nor crying, neither shall there be any more pain: for the former things are passed away." Neither shall there be any more chains, no more heartaches, fear, loneliness, insecurity, hatred, poverty, or persecution. You will be free at last!

Speaker: (releases handcuffs, unwinds chains, and lets them drop to the floor): Free at last! Oh, how I long for that day! *(Give a personal testimony of* one *thing that you will be glad to be rid of when Jesus comes. Make it something personal that relates to you or your family. What are you longing to be free from more than anything else? Death, a wheelchair, pain, trips to the doctor?)* Praise God! When Jesus comes, I won't have that to worry about anymore! I will be free at last!

Leader: I know that you too are longing for that glorious day of freedom when Jesus comes. What more than anything else do *you* wish to be free from? What are the chains that Jesus is going to take away from you, from your loved ones, from this old world that will make you shout for joy when He returns?

I am coming down into the congregation now with a roving mike. This is your opportunity to tell what you are looking forward to being without when Jesus comes. Who'll be first? Please raise your hand, and I'll bring the mike to you. *(People will respond, but don't hesitate to walk over to people and ask them directly to respond. Take five to seven minutes for these testimonies. Ad lib as you go from person to person so that there are no "dead" moments. Talk about the glories of that moment when Jesus comes and the freedom that will be ours at last.)*

Won't it be glorious when all our labors and trials are over and we are safe on that beautiful shore? Oh, that will be glory for me—when I am free at last. What about you? Let's join our hearts in singing "The Glory Song," No. 435 in *The SDA Hymnal.*

CONGREGATIONAL SONG

Our brothers and sisters in _____ are also looking forward to that glorious day when they will be free at last. _____ has a report from there right now.

MISSION REPORT

The Supermarket

6

Preparation

Move the pulpit to the far side of the platform. Place a sign on it that says "The Supermarket." Center a long table on the platform to serve as the checkout counter. Have a pile of brown bags at one end. In a nearby box have boxes and bottles bearing the following labels: TRUST, FORGIVENESS, SHARING, SMILES AND A SONG, APPRECIATION, GRACE, QUIET TIME, and HOPE. *(Use common items found in a supermarket, such as cereal, detergent, paper towels, etc.)*

Have a similar set of grocery items for the negative emotions so that a person can exchange a cereal box that says "Pessimism" for another cereal box that says "Hope." The negative product labels should be: DOUBT, ANGER, SELF-PITY, DEPRESSION, CRITICISM, SIN, GUILT, FRUSTRATIONS, and PESSIMISM. Place the negative products on the front pews.

Borrow some shopping baskets from a local store. Store uniforms would enhance the program but are not necessary.

The Parable of the Supermarket

(Note: A pantomime of the following narrative would make the parable more effective but is not required.)

Narrator: Verily, verily, I say unto you that the kingdom of heaven is like unto a businessman who receiveth a franchise for the local supermarket, which when he hath filled it with all manner of produce for the good of humanity, doth advertise for customers to come and buy.

And lo, while his employees slept, a salesman for a rival chain cometh and placeth his brand of merchandise upon the shelves, making sure that his prices are less than those of the company's brand.

When the employees of the supermarket discovered the false merchandise, they sought out the manager and findeth him at the front doors, ready to unlock them for the first customers.

"Good sir," the employees saith unto him, "an enemy salesman has come into the store in the night and placed his merchandise upon your shelves. Behold, it is everywhere and much lower priced than our brand. Shall we, therefore, keep the store closed while we seek to remove the enemy's brand?"

Then spake the Good Manager unto His employees, saying, "Nay, not so. For lift up thine eyes and behold—the customers are already waiting to enter. The time is at hand. I must open the doors. Leave the merchandise on the shelves, and let the customers choose, for perchance they may be able to distinguish between the good and the evil."

"But, Good Manager," remonstrated the clerks, "what if they cannot?"

Then spake the Good Manager, "Fear not, for it shall be that when they come to the cash register, you shall point out their mistake and exchange the false merchandise for the true."

And so it was that the clerks obeyed the Good Manager. They took their places at the checkout counter, and the doors were opened. The customers entered to make their selections.

(Customers enter. Pick up shopping baskets. Make selections from front pews and line up at the checkout table in numerical order. Clerk and bagger take place behind table.)

Customer 3: Wow! Look at the bargains! SELF-PITY! Just what I've been needing!

Customer 4: Did you see this? You can get two packets of DEPRESSION for the price of one! I might as well stock up!

Customer 2: This ANGER is the least expensive I've seen anywhere! I never know when I might need some! My husband is always coming up with something to upset me.

Customer 6: Look at this bargain! For every SIN, they're giving away a free packet of GUILT!

Customer 7: I can't believe it! They're practically giving away

FRUSTRATION!

Customer 1: After what happened to me this week, DOUBT is just what I need!

Customer 5: CRITICISM at an 80 percent discount! I've received plenty this week, and now I can pay it back in kind!

Customer 8: PESSIMISM—my favorite way to start the day! I'll buy two boxes—just to make sure I don't run out!

(By this time everyone should be lined up at the checkout counter. One at a time they place their purchases on the counter—label facing the congregation. After the exchange product is accepted, the bagger puts it in a paper sack and the customer leaves.)

Clerk: Excuse me, but are you sure that DOUBT is what you want?

Customer 1: Of course! Do you know what happened to me this week? I lost my job! It's not fair, I tell you. God could have done something about it, but He didn't. I'm beginning to wonder if He really cares. Getting a job is not easy. I've prayed and nothing has happened. I sometimes wonder if He even exists. Yes, DOUBT is just what I feel like doing.

Bagger: TRUST really works better. It's hard for us to understand why bad things happen to us, but trust believes that "all things work together for good" to those who love the Lord. He has promised to never leave or forsake those who TRUST in Him. Won't you give it a try?

Customer 1: Thank you. I think I will. *(Pushes away DOUBT. Bagger puts TRUST in the bag.)*

Clerk: It looks like you plan to use a lot of ANGER.

Customer 2: You'd need ANGER too, if you had *my* husband and kids to live with! They've done plenty in the past to make me upset, and I expect they will in the future, too, so I'm ready for them with plenty of ANGER.

Clerk: ANGER really doesn't help, you know. It only makes things worse.

Bagger: FORGIVENESS works wonders! I'd try it if I were you. I know it's hard to believe, but I've seen whole families changed with the use of FORGIVENESS. There's enough here to make at least 490 applications.

Customer 2: Really? Four hundred ninety? That's 70 times 7. Seems I remember Jesus saying something about forgiving that many times. OK, I'll take it!

Clerk: If it hasn't worked after 490 applications, come back and we'll give you another bottle free!

Customer 3: I have such a hard life. Poor little old me! Nobody has to suffer the things I've had to endure! I can't begin to tell you how much I need this SELF-PITY.

Clerk: I hate to tell you this, but SELF-PITY only makes you feel worse. It's addicting, too. The more you use, the more you want. Look around you. Be honest. There are lots of people with problems, many of them worse off than you.

Bagger: What you need is a good dose of SHARING. When you try to help others by sharing their burden, it makes your own heart lighter. Honestly.

Clerk: If you'll use SHARING to help make someone else happy, you'll find your troubles getting smaller.

Customer 3: I think you've got a point. I'll give it a try. *(Turns to congregation as he walks away.)* You know, I have more green beans than I know what to do with. I think I'll share some with my next-door neighbor who was in an accident and couldn't plant a garden this year.

Customer 4: (Sighing, then drooping shoulders): Oh, I feel so depressed. Nothing ever turns out right. I'm a loser, that's what I am! There's no hope for me.

Clerk: Oh, but there is! You don't have to take more DEPRESSION home!

Customer 4: (Sighing): It's OK. I'm used to it. *(Sighs again.)*

Bagger: Why don't you give SMILES AND A SONG a try? This brand will really make you feel much better.

Customer 4: I don't feel like smiling and singing. I feel like being depressed.

Clerk: But SMILES AND A SONG have a magic ingredient that will make you feel happier! Come on, just try it. Smile for me!

Customer 4 (Smiling): You know what? I do feel better! You can keep the DEPRESSION. I'll go for SMILES AND A SONG after this!

Clerk: SMILES AND A SONG—a good choice for everyone! Let's all make that choice right now. Let's sing "Praise Him! Praise Him!" number 249 in *The SDA Hymnal.* And let's smile as we sing it!

OPENING SONG

PRAYER

Clerk: You certainly want a lot of CRITICISM!

Customer 5: You've got it wrong! I don't *want* CRITICISM. I want to *give it back* to all those who have criticized me! I'm ready to get even.

Bagger: And they'll return the CRITICISM, so what progress have you made? Wouldn't you rather make friends than enemies?

Customer 5: If they wanted to be my friends, they wouldn't have criticized me in the first place!

Clerk: Try some of our APPRECIATION brand. It has a way of wiping out criticism. It actually turns enemies into friends.

Customer 5: You don't say? That sounds terrific! But how do you use it on people who have so many faults?

Bagger: Everybody has some redeeming feature. Look for the good in everyone—and appreciate *that.* Ignore what you don't like. Praise what you do like. You'll find the good growing and the bad shrinking. APPRECIATION actually gets rid of faults.

Customer 5: Good! Give me lots of APPRECIATION. I have plenty of people I need to try it on!

Clerk: I think all of us need to practice using the APPRECIA- TION brand. Please stand up and look around you. Find at least three people whom you can use it on. Appreciate something specific about that person. It might be the smile, the way he or she is dressed, or something he or she has done for you recently. Get out your appreciation, and put it to work on three people right now.

ONE-TO-ONE SHARING

Clerk: Surely you don't want to carry around that heavy box of GUILT.

Customer 6: But it's free! I'm not one to pass up something free, even if it is heavy!

Clerk: Oh, but you didn't read the fine print. GUILT isn't really free. You'll pay in sickness, pain, heartache, and sorrow as long as you have it. If you hang on to it long enough, you'll pay with your life, for the wages of SIN is death.

Customer 6: Oh, that's not a very good deal at all!

Bagger: Try GRACE instead. God's GRACE will forgive all your sins the moment you confess them. God's GRACE will bury your sins in the depths of the sea, and He will remember them no more. God's GRACE will bring you joy, peace, and eternal life.

Customer 6: GRACE is all I need!

Customer 7: I really don't want all these FRUSTRATIONS either. I've been reading the fine print. They cause ulcers and high blood pressure!

Clerk: You're right! We have something much better. It's called QUIET TIME. To use this, you need to spend some time alone with God every day, reading His Word, praying, and thinking about Him. Taking a walk in nature also helps. Our FRUSTRATIONS vanish as we spend time with God.

Customer 7: That's exactly what I need, some QUIET TIME!

Clerk: Do you always start your day with PESSIMISM?

Customer 8: Oh, yes! How else can you begin the day? The world is in such a mess! There's trouble in the Middle East, trouble in Central America, trouble in Europe, and trouble in the White House! There's even trouble in the church. I used to think the Lord was coming soon, but now I don't see how He can. We aren't doing what we should be doing!

Clerk: What you need is some HOPE. You need to cheer up and look on the bright side. There are a lot of good things going on in this world. God is still in control! He's at work in many lands. The

44

church is growing and prospering!

Customer 8: Like where?

Bagger: Like in _____ . Why don't you just sit down for a moment and listen to _____ give a report of the work over there? I think it will cheer you up!

MISSION REPORT

Customer 8: You know, the Lord *is* at work! With Him in control, there *is* HOPE. *(Takes bag of HOPE and leaves.)*

Narrator: And it shall come to pass that at closing time the Good Manager will remove the false merchandise from the supermarket shelves and throw it into the trash container. Then the garbage truck will come and take it all away so that these things will never again tempt the customers. Bad merchandise shall not fill the shelves a second time!

Until that day, I say unto you, Watch and pray that ye buy not the wrong merchandise!

Quiz Program

Survival Kit for Single Women

7

Preparation

On a table on the platform, display a large first-aid kit, tool box, or other box labeled in large letters: "Survival Kit for Single Women." Inside the kit place cards with the following words printed large enough for the congregation to read: "Hope," "Faith," "Networking," "Acceptance," "Guidance," "Friendship." *(Cards may be made as stand-up display cards for the table or backed with a strip of sandpaper and used on a flannel board.)*

(While Bible costumes are not essential, they would make the program more effective. The Bible women could be sitting in the congregation and come up as needed, or they could come in from the side rooms as called. At the appropriate time each woman opens the survival kit, takes out a word, and displays it so the congregation can read it.)

For the song service, plan only songs written by single women. The following songs are from *The SDA Hymnal*: Anne Steele, No. 15; Annie R. Smith, Nos. 439, 441, 447; Charlotte Elliot, Nos. 313, 314, 603; and Frances Ridley Havergal, Nos. 74, 281, 316, 330, 535, 541.

Program

Narrator: On Monday the people of the United States will celebrate Memorial Day. We [they] will remember brave heroes of battle and loved ones who lie in thousands of quiet, green cemeteries—heroes and dear ones whom God has not forgotten.

There is another group of people whom God remembers but we often forget—the single women in our church and community. This group of widows, divorcees, students, single parents, and single professionals have special needs that the church family often overlooks or ignores. And though *we* may forget, God does not. Today we will meet six single women whom God remembered. Perhaps as we listen we will find ways that we too can remember this very special group among us. They will share items from the Survival Kit for Single Women, which can help you or a friend survive in today's difficult world of singles.

Networking

Ruth: I was left a widow at an early age. Worse still, I had no child. In the ancient Near East this meant I had no status, no inheritance, no home, no place, and no income. I was in desperate straits. My only hope was remarriage, but widows weren't much in demand. I looked at the young virgins who were laughing and dancing in the villages, and I envied them their youth, their desirability, and their hope of a future. Times had been good, but now they were bad—real bad. I had come to the end of my rope. How could I survive?

Narrator: Who was this widow from Moab? *(Get response from audience: Ruth.)* Ruth, tell us, how *did* you survive?

Ruth (taking "Networking" out of survival kit): Networking did it for me. Alone, I could never have made it as a widow. I joined forces with my mother-in-law, Naomi. She was a great support to me. She encouraged me to go to work and make friends, which I did. I got acquainted with the rich landowners in Bethlehem as well as with the hired hands. One contact led to another, and soon I was introduced to Boaz. And, well, you know the rest of the story. There was a proposal and marriage, with a bit of help from Naomi and God. I even had to make the first move, just to give Boaz the idea, you know. But it worked! I know that God helps singles build networks and then use them.

Narrator: And that's where you and I come in. It takes *people* like us to help build networks for singles. We can be part of the network of single women's lives, helping them succeed in the marketplace, helping them make the contacts they need.

Acceptance
Dinah: I was a young single looking for a good time. Life was boring in my father's tents. I dressed in my finest and went out into the world, where the excitement was. I went out to meet the daughters of the land and have fun. And did I ever have fun! The daughters had brothers! One in particular, Shechem, was so handsome and so kind. Before I knew it, we had gone to bed together. Among my people my loss of virginity was a terrible disgrace. I began to feel used, soiled, shamed. I'd never get a husband after what I had done, not a good man anyway. And I knew my folks would never let me marry Shechem, even though he said he wanted to. That, too, would be a disgrace, for he was a heathen. It was terrible. I wished I could die!

Narrator: Who was this young lady who felt disgraced? *(Dinah)* Yes, Dinah, you wanted to die, but you survived! Tell us how.

Dinah (taking out the "Acceptance" sign): It was the love and acceptance of my family that saw me through. Sure, I had done wrong. I shouldn't have gone where I went. I was asking for trouble—and I got it! But my family didn't disown me. They stood by me and fought for my honor. I felt really loved and part of the family again.

Narrator: There are millions of singles in 199– who, like Dinah, have rejected their spiritual heritage and gotten themselves into trouble. If they don't find the acceptance and love they need within the church, they will look for it outside of the family of God, for they must have it to survive. But all of us can help supply unconditional love and acceptance. You and I can be the family that many singles need.

Faith
Widow of Zarephath: My husband died, leaving me with a young son to raise. We worked hard and somehow managed to eat, but then the famine came. We were down to our last handful of flour and our last few drops of oil. I went outside the village to gather a few sticks. I would make a fire, bake a little bread, eat it with my

son—and die. With a heavy heart I began to gather those sticks. It's a terrible thing to watch your son—your pride and joy, the hope of your old age—grow weak from lack of food. His shiny black hair had become coarse, dry, and brittle. His eyes had sunk into his head. His skin was hanging from his bones, and I wanted so much to see him happy and healthy again. I wanted so much to give him food, but there was none to give.

Narrator: Does anyone recognize this distraught widow? *(Widow of Zarephath)* Tell us, how did you survive?

Widow of Zarephath: By my faith. *(Takes "Faith" from the kit.)* Just when I had come to the end of my resources, God sent Elijah the prophet to ask me for food. How could I give the last meal for my son to a man who looked strong and healthy? Yet that man was God's servant. I knew that God was asking me to do it. Elijah promised me that my barrel of flour would not go empty and my cruse of oil would not go dry. It took a lot of faith to do it, but I obeyed. And from that moment on, God supplied all the food we needed. I know you can depend on God when you can depend on no one else.

Narrator: Yes, of course! God supplies the physical needs of the singles among us, but often He does it through us. Perhaps today God is telling you of a single who needs some financial help, just a little boost to see her through a very difficult situation. What a privilege to be an Elijah helping to supply the needs of singles!

Hope

Hagar: Do you have any idea what it's like to be rejected by your husband, to be sent out of the place that has been your home, to be left to raise a son alone? It's no joke being a single parent! The bills pile up, and the chariot needs fixing. The plumbing goes on the blink, and the roof needs repair. How's a woman to manage all alone? But the worst part are those lonely nights when you wonder what it is about you that is so unattractive that he rejected you and sent you packing. When it happened to me, I felt that I'd rather die than go on. There was no way I could raise a teenager alone. There was no way I could cope. I didn't even want to try.

Narrator: Who could this single parent be? *(Hagar)* Tell us,

Hagar, how did you manage?

Hagar: I managed because the Lord gave me hope. *(Takes out "Hope" from survival kit.)* He came to me in the desert and told me that He would make a great nation of my son, Ishmael. He promised not to leave us. He helped me raise my son and get him married. Without hope I could not have survived.

Narrator: Do you know a single parent to whom you could give a little hope? What about it, men? Could you find some fatherless boys to take along on a camping trip? Might there be a single parent and her children whom you could include in your Sabbath afternoon fellowship? Single mothers have a difficult time because of baby-sitting problems. Is there a grandmother in Israel who could relieve one of these single mothers occasionally so she could come to a meeting or just go shopping unhindered?

Guidance

Eunice: I too was a single parent with a son to raise. My husband had provided well enough for me, but what I needed was wisdom in how to raise my boy. My husband's people, among whom I lived at Lystra, were Gentiles. I was having a hard time raising my son to be a Jew, and then my mother and I became Christians, and life got even more complicated. Where could I turn for help? I wanted my son to grow up to work for Jesus, but I felt so inadequate at times. The temptations of the world were out there, and I feared for my young son's future.

Narrator: Does anyone know this single parent and her mother and son? *(Eunice, Lois, and Timothy)* You did a wonderful job raising Timothy, Eunice. How did you do it?

Eunice: I could never have done it alone! I needed guidance. *(Takes "Guidance" from survival kit.)* And I got it from Paul and the other members of the Christian fellowship in Lystra. Those people saw me through the difficult times.

Narrator: I wonder if we are doing everything we can do for the young single mothers in our church and community? Surely we have a responsibility to help bring up the children of single-parent families in the nurture and admonition of the Lord.

Friendship

Woman taken in adultery: I found out rather quickly that once you make a mistake, it seems as though the whole church sits in judgment. Oh, how the censure hurts! Words can pierce deeper than arrows! Words can bruise more than stones, for they can reach the heart! And the embarrassment and humiliation! I lay in the dust before my accusers and wished they would stop talking and start throwing their stones.

Narrator: Who was the woman in the dust? *(Woman taken in adultery)* But those stones were never thrown. You regained your self-respect, and in the Gospels you have a place of honor. What happened?

Woman taken in adultery: I had found a friend! *(Takes "Friendship" out of kit.)* A Friend who believed in me! A Friend who refused to judge me! One such friend can make a difference, especially when that friend is Jesus! I would advise all single women. Make Him your very best friend. Sit at His feet every day. He will restore your self-esteem. He will help you forgive those who have wronged you. He will make life worth living once more!

Narrator: I too can be a friend of single women! I too can refuse to judge! I too can make a difference! What about you?

Single women have contributed much to the Christian church. They have been teachers, preachers, leaders, directors, nurses, doctors, organizers, and writers. Several hymns in our hymnal were written by single women.

One of these hymn writers, young Frances Havergal, stood in the art gallery in Dusseldorf, Germany, and gazed at the face of Christ in the painting entitled "Behold the Man." As she stared at the crown of thorns and the blood trickling down Jesus' brow, she wished she could wipe His forehead and comfort Him. Somehow she must put into words the loneliness she saw in that face. As Frances Havergal stared at the painting, it was as if Christ were trying to get her to understand the terrible agony He endured.

Pulling an old circular from her pocket, Frances quickly scribbled down the words of a poem and returned the paper to her pocket. Later it was set to music. It is No. 281 in *The SDA Hymnal*—"I

Gave My Life for Thee." May each single woman here today find in it a message of hope and love.

SPECIAL MUSIC: "I Gave My Life for Thee"

PRAYER

Scripted Panel

The Ideal Way to Solve Problems

---------------------- **8** ----------------------

Preparation

Before Sabbath school begins, place the letters of the word IDEAL on the chalkboard vertically. They will be used as an acrostic for today's program.

Program

Welcome to Sabbath school! Have you had a good week? Or has it been a week of difficult decisions and confusing choices? Aren't you thankful for the Sabbath, a time we can push aside the problems of the week and gain a new perspective for the week to come? Our opening song this morning speaks of that Sabbath rest and renewal.

OPENING SONG: *(Choose a Sabbath hymn.)*

PRAYER

Superintendent: We can lay aside our problems for a few hours of the Sabbath, but sooner or later we must face them. Decisions constantly must be made to settle differences that arise in our homes, in our workplace, and in the church. How can we find the IDEAL solution to our problems? That is the topic of our Sabbath school this morning. Listen in! Perhaps you'll find something to help you in the decisions you face.

Problem-solving Panel

Leader: It was near the end of the grading period. The students' industrial arts projects would soon be due. Mark and Steve were both involved with complicated projects, and each needed to use a special clamp. But the shop had only one of these clamps. Both Mark and Steve were anxious to get a good grade. Each decided that he should be the one to use the clamp first. The result was a fight in the hall while a circle of classmates cheered. A teacher finally separated the guys. It was now his job to resolve the conflict. They were expecting him to solve the problem. How would *you* solve it if you were in his shoes? What is the IDEAL solution? *(Point to word on chalkboard.)* I've called in a panel of three experts to help us, men and women experienced in helping solve problems. So, experts, what would you do in this situation?

Expert 1: The very first step is to *identify the problem. (Fill in the "I" of the acrostic.)* The problem is not that Mark is angry at Steve. It is not even that the guys are fighting in the hall. The problem is that there is only one clamp, and both cannot use it at the same time.

Expert 2: You're so right! When identifying the problem we must be careful to not look at emotions or actions but at the need that caused the emotions and actions. Always define a problem in terms of *needs*. We must ask, What is the basic need here? In this case it is time available for using the clamp.

Expert 3: The second step is to *describe the options. (Fill in the "D" of the acrostic.)* Brainstorm in a group for all possible solutions. All suggestions are accepted, no matter how zany they may sound. The object is to get as many ideas as possible. We are after quantity, not quality. No evaluation takes place. Make a list of all ideas.

Expert 1: Nobody says, "No!" Nobody says, "That won't work!" Nobody says, "That's a stupid idea!" Nobody says, "That will cost too much." Nobody says, "We've already tried that." Nobody even says, "That's a terrific idea!" Absolutely no evaluation must take place while ideas are being listed.

Expert 3: In the case of Mark and Steve, the group came up with the following possible solutions:

    a. Mark would complete his project first, then Steve.

    b. Steve would complete his project first, then Mark.

    c. One or both could change to a different project.

    d. Get another clamp.

    e. One or both could drop the course.

THE IDEAL WAY TO SOLVE PROBLEMS

f. A schedule would be worked out to allow both students to share the clamp for an equal amount of time.

Expert 2: Once all the options are listed, it is time to *evaluate. (Fill in the "E" of the acrostic.)* Now is the time to express opinions about each item listed. Which items are completely unacceptable? Which items are not possible? Which item appears to meet everyone's needs in the best way? Continue discussion until one item is selected with the consent of everyone in the group.

Expert 1: In the case of Mark and Steve, both a and b were found to be unworkable because there was not enough time remaining in the term to complete first one project and then the other. Item c was ruled out for lack of time. Item e was ruled out because neither was willing to drop out. Both Mark and Steve wanted item d, but it was discovered that the clamp had to be ordered from out of town and that it would take three weeks for delivery. Only two weeks were left in the term. All agreed that item f was the only possible alternative. A daily schedule was set up allowing each student equal time on the clamp.

Expert 1: The next step was to *assign* and *act. (Fill in the "A" of the acrostic.)* After a decision is reached, it is important to decide who will be responsible for carrying out the action. In this case Mark and Steve were to give the teacher a list of their free periods, and the teacher would make out a schedule. The schedule was approved by both guys.

Expert 3: The next step toward an ideal solution is to *learn from your decision.* This means further evaluation after the solution is implemented. How did it go? Was it a good decision? What can we learn from it to help us in the future?

Expert 2: In the case of Mark and Steve, the evaluation took place at the end of the marking period. Both finished their projects on time, and both received high grades. They remained friends. There were no more fights over the clamp. They were satisfied with the results of the problem-solving process.

Expert 3: Let's review the process for arriving at an IDEAL solution to a group problem.

I —Identify the problem in terms of needs.

D—Describe the options. Brainstorm without evaluation.

E—Evaluate the solutions suggested. Arrive at an acceptable solution.

A—Appoint someone to carry out the decision. Act.

L—Learn from the decision. Evaluate the outcome.

Leader: Thank you, panel of experts. I'm looking forward to having an opportunity to try the IDEAL method of problem-solving. I can see many applications for it at home, at school, and at work. It could be used to make plans for a group, to help with relationships, and in individual problem-solving as well. I can imagine using this method to decide on a variety of things ranging from what I should do next summer to what color the new church carpet should be.

In following the IDEAL method of problem-solving, we are obeying the words of Scripture to "live peaceably with all men" (Rom. 12:18).

We are not alone in having difficult decisions to make. We are not alone in having problems that are difficult to solve. The problems that our brothers and sisters face in mission lands make some of ours seem insignificant. Today we have a report about some of the difficult decisions that must be faced in _____.

MISSION REPORT

Skits

A Different Kind
of Music

———————— 9 ————————

Preparation

Franklin E. Belden, nephew of Ellen G. White, was a prominent songwriter among early Adventists. He was one of the music editors of *Hymns and Tunes*, published in 1886. Later he was a superintendent at the Review and Herald Publishing House. He wrote hundreds of Sabbath school songs and hymns, in most cases the words as well as the music. Twelve of these are in *The SDA Hymnal*. Twenty-four can be found in *The Church Hymnal*. *(Use only songs written by F. E. Belden for the song service.)*

Display a poster that reads "Adventist 20/20." Arrange for two mikes, one on opposite corners of the platform, saving center stage for pantomime skits depicting early Adventist history. *(While this program is more effective with the skits, it can be done without them, letting the congregation imagine the scenes.)* Plan to have only two verses sung for each song or special number or the program will be too long.

Program

Reporter 1: Happy Sabbath! And welcome to the studios of *Adventist 20/20!*

Reporter 2: The program that answers questions you have been asking!

Reporter 1: Meet your reporters, _____. *(Name of reporter 2. Gestures toward reporter 2.)*

Reporter 2: And ——————— . *(Name of reporter 1. Gestures* *toward reporter 1.)* Today we are investigating our Adventist musical roots.

Reporter 1: Our topic is "A Different Kind of Music," music with an Adventist flavor.

Skit 1: 1831, Low Hampton, New York

(As story is told, William Miller, carrying a folding chair and Bible, walks onto center stage. He sits down and begins to turn the pages of his Bible, taking notes as he studies. Prays. Nephew enters. Miller unrolls chart of 2300 days. Exits with chair.)

Reporter 2: Our search begins in Low Hampton, New York. It is early August 1831. Fifty-year-old William Miller is searching the Scriptures. As he reads again the verses that tell of Christ's soon return he is overwhelmed with the conviction that God is calling him to tell this message to others. He appears troubled. William Miller is not a preacher, but a farmer. Is God really calling him? Would anyone listen to him?

"Dear Lord, is this really a call from You? If it is, then please send someone to ask me to preach. If You do that, I will go."

(Enter nephew. Knocks. Miller rises. Pantomime conversation.)

A few moments later there is a knock on his door. It is his nephew, Irving Guilford, from the nearby town of Dresden. "Father sent me to ask you to come and preach at our place tomorrow morning. We want you to tell us about what you have studied on the second coming of Christ." *(Nephew exits.)*

William Miller was stunned. He had not really expected an invitation to preach. After spending some time in the maple grove beside his house, he surrendered to God's call. That afternoon he made the 16-mile journey to Dresden.

The following morning, probably August 7, William Miller stood up to preach before a congregation gathered in the kitchen of the Guilford home.

People were electrified. Only 12 more years! Whole families gave their hearts to the Lord.

Soon invitations poured in from many places. Thousands of people accepted the message that Jesus was coming in 1843 or 1844.

A DIFFERENT KIND OF MUSIC

A song on many lips was "How Sweet Are the Tidings."

OPENING SONG: "How Sweet Are the Tidings," No. 442, *The SDA Hymnal*

PRAYER

Reporter 1: One of those who responded to the preaching of William Miller was a 21-year-old schoolteacher from Palmyra, Maine, James White, member of a musical family, his father having been at one time a voice teacher.

In the autumn of 1843 James White, his father, and two of his sisters attended the Maine Eastern Christian Conference, to be held in the town of Knox. A storm caused them to spend the night in a wayside tavern. That evening the landlord and his guests were entertained by the White Second Advent Quartet singing songs of the coming of Jesus. In the morning the proprietor canceled their bill and invited them to make his place their home whenever they passed that way.

One of the songs they might have sung that night was "Never Part Again."

SPECIAL MUSIC: "Never Part Again," No. 449, *The SDA Hymnal. (If possible, have it sung by a mixed quartet. Alternative: congregational song.)*

Reporter 2: On the last day of the Knox Conference several ministers urged James White to speak.

Feeling his immaturity and recognizing that at the final meeting the best man among them should give the message, he withdrew from the meeting to pray for guidance.

Finally he decided that he would go in and walk toward the front. Then if the ministers there invited him, he would speak.

Skit 2: 1843, Knox, Maine
(Three ministers take seats on platform. Center one should be

67

an older man with large Bible open on his lap. James White walks down center aisle. Two men rise, go to meet him, and escort him to the platform. White takes Bible and looks up texts, then rises to speak.)

Reporter 2: Entering the meeting place, James saw an older minister sitting in the center of the platform. Clearly the man was prepared to speak. As James neared the platform, his brother Samuel and another minister stepped down to meet him. Taking hold of his arms, they escorted him to the platform. At his direction, his brother Samuel announced a hymn. Then prayer was offered. At the end of the prayer the Bible was on James White's lap, and he was hurriedly looking up the texts for his sermon.

After another song he moved forward while hearty amens rang through the hall. He preached a mighty sermon on the Second Coming, following which the Lord's Supper was administered.

While the table was being set for this, James White and his sisters sang, "You Will See Your Lord a-Coming," punctuated with shouts of "Glory!" from the congregation. Many were in tears, while responses of amen and "Praise the Lord!" resounded through the meeting place.

SPECIAL MUSIC: "You Will See Your Lord a-Coming," No. 438, *The SDA Hymnal. (Try to get a trio for this number. Alternate plans would be to have a male solo or have the congregation sing.)*

Reporter 1: We take you now to Somerville, Massachusetts, near Boston. The year is 1851.

One Friday night Annie R. Smith decided to attend meetings held by Elder Joseph Bates. That night she dreamed of arriving late and taking a seat at the door. A man whom she had never seen was standing on the platform. He was pointing to a chart and saying, "Unto two thousand three hundred days, then shall the sanctuary be cleansed."

On that same night Elder Bates dreamed that at the last minute he changed his topic. Then just as he began, the door opened and a strange woman entered. He took her at once to be Sister Smith's daughter, Annie.

Skit 3: 1851, Somerville, Massachusetts

(Elder Bates takes place on platform, facing choir loft and holding Bible and chart. Annie Smith enters and sits in seat farthest from preacher. Afterward she comes forward to center stage, and the two shake hands and pantomime conversation.)

Reporter 1: The next day Annie started out for the meeting with plenty of time to spare, but lost her way and arrived late. She opened the door and found every seat filled except for one near the door. She sat down just as Elder Bates began to speak. He pointed to a chart and said, "Unto two thousand three hundred days, then shall the sanctuary be cleansed."

I can't believe it! Annie thought. *It's exactly as I dreamed it would be! He's preaching the truth.*

Amazing! Elder Bates thought as he looked up to see the door open and the girl in his dream take a seat by the door. He had forgotten about his dream when he stood up to preach. He had another topic in mind, then for some reason switched it to the message about the 2300 days and the sanctuary truth. After the meeting Elder Bates shook Annie's hand and said, "You must be Sister Smith's daughter. I dreamed of you last night."

"And I dreamed of you and what you preached tonight!" Annie exclaimed. "I believe it is the truth."

(Exit Bates and Annie Smith.)

Annie R. Smith became an editorial worker for the Review and Herald. She also wrote the words for three songs in *The SDA Hymnal*, Nos. 339, 441, and 447. Let's join our voices now in singing No. _____.

CONGREGATIONAL SONG: *(Choose one of Annie R. Smith's songs.)*

Skit 4: 1915, St. Helena, California

(Pantomime the bedroom scene with doctor examining Mrs. White.)

SABBATH SCHOOL PROGRAM PLANNER

Reporter 2: Come with me now to Elmshaven, near St. Helena, California. It is February 13, 1915. A doctor is bent over the bed of a frail, elderly woman and appears to be carefully examining her. He straightens and shakes his head. He has discovered a break in her left hip. Since she is 87, it cannot be expected to heal.

After giving directions for her care, Dr. G. E. Klingerman returns to St. Helena Sanitarium on the hill above Elmshaven, where he had been on duty when called that Sabbath morning to attend to Mrs. Ellen White.

Sister White had fallen while entering her study. Her niece, May Walling, was nearby. She helped her aunt from the floor to the bed, where she was lying when the doctor came. Her death came five months later.

Even though ill, Mrs. White was always cheerful and happy. Again and again, during the earlier weeks of her illness, she often lifted her voice in song. The song she most often sang was No. 453 in *The SDA Hymnal*, "We Have Heard."

SPECIAL MUSIC: Lady's solo, "We Have Heard," No. 453, *The SDA Hymnal*. *(Alternative suggestion: use as a congregational song.)*

Reporter 1: Yes, we have heard of the bright, the holy land; we have heard and our hearts are glad! But what about the millions of people who have never heard? What are we doing to take the message of Christ's soon return to the millions in the _____ Division? Listen now as _____ brings a report from _____.

MISSION REPORT

Adventist Missions Today

10

Preparation

For two weeks before the program, insert the following announcement in your bulletin: "Channel 7, SDA Cable TV, will broadcast live *Adventist Missions Today* at 9:30 a.m. on Sabbath, _____ (date). Don't miss seeing your children and youth on TV! Your place in the studio audience is reserved."

On one side of platform place a table with a microphone for the two news anchors. They will remain seated throughout the program. Other speakers and actors will perform on the opposite side of the platform. Prepare two TV "cameras" from cardboard boxes (or borrow some video camcorders). Place on tripods, one on each side of the platform. Give cameramen earphones to wear. They stand there during the whole performance, pretending to take pictures of what is happening.

Program

Announcer (from hidden mike): This is channel 7, your friendly SDA Cable TV Network, with news of the Adventist Church around the world. Today's program is broadcast live from the _____ Adventist Church.

Organist (swell up and under): "Far and Near the Fields Are Teeming."

Anchor 1: Hello! Welcome to *Adventist Missions Today*, an exciting half hour of gospel news. Today we explore the countries that make up the Far Eastern Division of the Seventh-day Adventist

71

Church.

Anchor 2: Bangladesh, Brunei, Cambodia, and Hong Kong . . .

(As each country is mentioned a primary child walks out bearing sign with the name of the country. The children line up across the front of the church, below the platform. If possible, dress each child in the costume of that country.)

Anchor 1: Indonesia, Japan, North and South Korea, and Laos . . .

Anchor 2: Macao, Malaysia, Myanmar, and the Philippines . . .

Anchor 1: Singapore, Sri Lanka, Thailand, and Vietnam . . .

Anchor 2: Guam and Taiwan.

Anchor 1: In these lands live more than 800 million people, most of whom are non-Christians.

(As each religion is mentioned, a primary child walks out holding a card bearing the name of that religion. Dress in costume, if possible.)

Anchor 2: They are Buddhists, Muslims, Hindus . . .

Anchor 1: Confucianists, Shintoists, and Taoists (pronounced with a D—Dowist, rhymes with cow) . . .

Anchor 2: In this vast division there is one Seventh-day Adventist for every 1,100 people.

Anchor 1: Compare that with the South Pacific Division, which has one Adventist for every 129 persons!

Anchor 2: Or the Eastern Africa Division, where the ratio is one to 189.

Anchor 1: In North America it is one Adventist to 214.

Anchor 2: And in South America, one in 314.

Anchor 1: Only in Euro-Africa with one to 1,480 and in Southern Asia with one to 4,978, is the ratio greater.

Anchor 2: In the Far East the harvest truly is ripe for reaping.

SPEECH CHOIR: "Ripe for the Harvest" *(Primaries)*

All: Ready and ripe for the harvest,
Group 1: Look on the golden grain.
Group 2: Beautiful, bright, and golden,
Group 1: Scattered along the plain.

All: Ready and ripe for the harvest,
Group 2: Watched by a Saviour's care,
Group 1: Souls that to Him are precious,
Group 2: Wait for the reapers there.
All: Gather them in rejoicing,
     Gather them day by day;
Group 1: Youth with its bloom and sunshine . . .
Group 2: Age with its locks of gray.
All: Gather them in, oh, hasten!
     Why are we standing here?
Group 1: Summer will soon be over;
Group 2: Winter is drawing near.
All: Up and away, O reapers!
     Great is the work to do,
     Many the souls that perish;
     Why are the toilers few?
          —Author Unknown

Organist *(music swells and falls. Children exit.)*

Announcer *(hidden mike):* "The harvest truly is plenteous, but the labourers are few; pray ye therefore the Lord of the harvest, that he will send forth labourers into his harvest" (Matt. 9:37, 38).

Organist: *(Music swells and falls.)*

Anchor 2: If that is your prayer too, please open your hymnal to No. 358 in the *SDA Hymnal*. We will stand and sing "Far and Near the Fields Are Teeming."

OPENING SONG

PRAYER: *(Remember projects in the Far East.)*

Announcer: You are tuned in to channel 7, SDA TV, broadcasting live from the _____ Adventist Church.

Anchor 1: Didn't you know? Haven't you heard?

Anchor 2: Hasn't anyone ever told you that literature evangelists are the advance guard of missions? Colporteurs were the first missionaries to enter almost all the countries of the Far Eastern Division.

Anchor 1: Didn't you know? Haven't you heard?

Anchor 2: Hasn't anyone ever told you about Abram La Rue? I'd like you to meet him. Here he comes now!

La Rue: I was once a seaman, but when I was converted as an old man I had a great longing to take the gospel to China. I wrote to the General Conference and offered my services, but they felt I really couldn't do much because of my age. Also, I had no qualifications. They wrote that I could work on one of the islands of the Pacific, but I'd have to pay my own way. Now, Hong Kong is close to China, so I went there. I supported myself by selling Adventist books.

Anchor 1: Could you speak Chinese?

La Rue: Oh, no! I sold my books to the English-speaking sailors who put into port. One of these sailors became an Adventist and took the message to Guam.

Anchor 2: Did you work only in Hong Kong?

La Rue: No, I was the first Adventist missionary in Malaysia, Japan, Sri Lanka, and Indonesia.

Anchor 2: You sure got around! *(La Rue exits.)*

Anchor 1: R. A. Caldwell sold the first Adventist books in the Philippines and in Thailand. Part of our offering today goes to help build the first Adventist college in Thailand.

Anchor 2: Chinese colporteurs were among the first to enter Vietnam, Taiwan, and Malaysia.

Anchor 1: Colporteurs from India began work in Bangladesh and Burma.

Anchor 2: Burma, now called Myanmar, is the country made famous by Eric B. Hare, author of the junior devotional *Make God First*. I love his *Jungle Stories* and *Treasure From the Haunted Pagoda*.

Anchor 1: Didn't you know? Haven't you heard? Hasn't anyone ever told you? Several years ago Adventist mission schools were closed by the government, but now we have discovered that we can operate seminaries. So we have extended the seminaries to include kindergarten through college.

Anchor 2: Yes, I've heard and I'm glad. We need those seminaries for bright Myanmar boys like Ta Wa. Remember how Eric B. Hare told it in *Jungle Heroes*?

Skit: Galvanized Iron

(Stage Setting: Teacher Chit Mg and children, dressed in simple cotton shirts and shorts or skirts, take their places. Children sit cross-legged on the floor behind benches that are placed in front of the teacher's desk. Hare [with hair parted in the middle and greased down] walks in and shakes hands with the teacher, who hands Hare the class record book.)

Narrator: Eric B. Hare is spending a week at the Awbawa outstation. It is the time of the half-yearly examinations.

Children (snapping to attention): Good morning, Thara.

Hare: Good morning, boys and girls. You may be seated. *(Opens record book and begins roll call.)* Bogale.

Bogale: Present, sir.

Hare: Dee Dee.

Dee Dee: Present, sir.

Hare: Naw Thu Ter.

Naw Thu Ter: Present, sir.

Hare: Ta Wa. *(Silence.)* Ta Wa! *(Silence. Looks up.)* Chit Mg, what's the matter with Ta Wa? Why is he not present?

Teacher: I'm afraid he's late, Thara.

Hare (looking into record book again; frowning, and shaking head): H'mmmm. *(Turns page.)* Late every day for three months! I shall certainly give Mr. Ta Wa a lecture the minute the first examination is over! Now it's time to begin.

Narrator (teacher passes out papers and pencils as narrator speaks; children pretend to take exam): The teacher passes out the examination papers, and the students begin their work. About halfway through the first period they hear someone running.

(Enter Ta Wa, running down an aisle, buttoning coat, and combing hair with his fingers. Scrambles onto the platform and takes a seat.)

Hare (hands on hips as he watches Ta Wa's entrance): Who's that?

Teacher: Ta Wa.

Hare: Ta Wa, you are late! See me after this examination!

Ta Wa: Yes, sir! Sorry, sir!

Hare (as though talking to himself): What a pity! A fine boy like that, late! What kind of man will he grow up to be?

Narrator: At last the examination is over and the boys go to recess. *(Boys hand papers to teacher and file out. Teacher leaves too. Only Ta Wa remains.)*

Hare (placing chair beside desk): Ta Wa, come here please. I want to have a little talk with you.

Ta Wa (coming forward and smiling): Yes, Thara.

Hare (clearing throat and looking stern): Ta Wa, my boy, I noticed you were late this morning. Furthermore, you have been late every day for three months now, so . . .”

Ta Wa (beaming and nodding): Yes, sir! I know it, but never mind. I am so very happy about it all. You see, I—

Hare (interrupting and waving hand in front of Ta Wa): Now, Ta Wa, boys who are always late for school and late for examinations will be late for work when they grow up, and late for everything. Maybe late for the kingdom, and—

Ta Wa (interrupting and smiling): But Thara, it doesn't matter about my being late. Because, you see, my parents don't want me to go to school at all. My father said I was lazy—trying to get out of work. So he said, "All right, you may go to school, but you will have to do your work before you go!"

So I get up in the morning at 3:00. I catch the bullocks and go to the paddy field. I have to plow in the dark. When the sun comes up, the village men come out to work. But my work is half done. When the sun is halfway up the heavens, my work is finished. I run home and grab my coat. I have to wash in a pool on the way to school. And I comb my hair with my fingers. Usually I'm one class late, but sometimes I'm only half a class late! My teacher helps me at night. And, Thara, I'm sure that I'll be able to pass my examination at the end of the year with the other children.

Hare: Ta Wa, I'm going to change your name.

Ta Wa: You are?

76

Hare: Yes, I'm going to put an *h* before the Ta and call you Hta Wa, because Hta Wa means "galvanized iron." A boy who can get up at 3:00 every day to get his work done is surely made of galvanized iron. It's good stuff, lad. You stick to it. One day God will make you a worker for Him.

(Exit Hare and Ta Wa.)

Anchor 1: Please give a generous offering so that many boys like Ta Wa can learn about Jesus.

Anchor 2: Please give liberally so that . . . *(Adapt to reflect current mission project.)*

Anchor 1: Please give to help . . . *(Adapt to reflect current mission project.)*

SPECIAL MUSIC: *(Cradle roll and/or kindergarten children sing one of their favorite offering songs.)*

OFFERING

Announcer (hidden mike): This is channel 7, SDA Cable TV, signing off for this week. Thank you for watching channel 7.

Surprise Programs

Pioneer Footprints

11

Preparation

Display a large map of the United States. Buy large colored gummed dot labels. Number seven dots. Place the dots on the map in the appropriate places to match the narration. Buy large white labels and write the following seven items on the labels: 1. William Miller, 2. Ellen White, 3. Joseph Bates, 4. *Adventist Review*, 5. J. N. Andrews, 6. Pitcairn, and 7. James White.

Take seven cards and label them Button 1, Button 2, etc. Tape these under seven chairs (pews) before the congregation arrives.

Decide on prizes to be given out.

Decorate the platform with antiques such as a spinning wheel, a covered wagon, patchwork quilts, and kerosene lamps. *(The leader could wear pioneer dress.)*

Program

Good morning and welcome to Pioneer Footprints, an exciting program that takes you backward in time to the beginning of the Seventh-day Adventist Church.

Come with me back to the days of covered wagons and kerosene lamps. Back to the days before computers and space shuttles. Long before TV and electricity. Back to the days of the horse and buggy, long dresses, high-topped buttoned shoes, and sun bonnets.

Are you ready to make the journey? Then fasten your seat belts and hold your breath, for we are about to hurtle back in time at the speed of 150 years per second!

Some of you are seated in chairs (pews) that are especially wired to activate our Sabbath school time machine. I will need the cooperation of everyone here to find the buttons that we need to place us in the early nineteenth century.

There are seven time machine buttons in all. Are you ready? Are you with me? Reach under your seat and feel for the button. It is a card taped to the chair (pew) bottom.

The seven of you who were lucky enough to find a card get to come up here and exchange it for a prize that is waiting for you. Of course, you will have to read whatever it says on your card or in your envelope. It isn't hard. If you can read, you can do it. What you read will tell us what happens next in our Sabbath school program.

So let's go! Number 1! Please come forward.

(Note: As each person comes forward to read what is on the card, you should be ready to put the label identifying the person or item talked about beside the correct numbered dot on the map.)

Time Machine Button 1

The time: 1831. The place: Dresden, New York. Fifty-year-old William Miller, a farmer, preached his first sermon to a congregation gathered in his sister's kitchen. He read from Daniel's prophecy about the 2300 days and explained that in prophecy one day equals one year. This prophecy began in 457 B.C. with the decree to rebuild Jerusalem. Subtracting this number from 2300, he got the year 1843. The date was later corrected to October 22, 1844.

Soon Miller was preaching to crowds of up to 10,000. People of all churches were expecting the Lord to come on October 22, 1844. They were disappointed, of course.

Although Adventists have learned not to set a specific date for Christ's return, we still believe that He is coming soon. Let's renew that hope as we sing a hymn loved by pioneer Adventists. *(Choose from Nos. 438 to 454 in* The SDA Hymnal.)

OPENING SONG

Time Machine Button 2

The year: 1844. The place: Portland, Maine. When Jesus failed to appear on October 22, 1844, the Harmon family was as much disappointed as any other Adventist family, but they did not give up their hope.

In December, while praying for light, Ellen Harmon, just 17 years old, had a vision. She told her friends: "I turned to look for the Advent people in the world, but could not find them, when a voice said to me, 'Look again, and look a little higher.' At this I raised my eyes, and saw a straight and narrow path, cast up high above the world. On this path the Advent people were traveling to the city which was at the farther end of the path."

Her attention was attracted to a "bright light set up behind them at the beginning of the path." As she looked at it, she heard the angel tell her that it was the "midnight cry." Here was the answer to their prayer. It was just what the disappointed Adventists needed. God is like that. He hears our prayers and gives us just the blessing we need.

Let's bow our heads just now and pray.

PRAYER

Time Machine Button 3

The time: 1845. The place: Fairhaven, Massachusetts. Joseph Bates, a retired sea captain, read about the seventh-day Sabbath in a Millerite paper. Deeply impressed, he traveled 140 miles to meet Frederick Wheeler. He arrived late, awakened the family, and studied with them the rest of the night. They then went on to the home of Cyrus Farnsworth and discussed the Sabbath truth until noon under his maple trees. Then Bates returned home.

Crossing the bridge between New Bedford and Fairhaven, he was hailed by James Madison M. Hall, a fellow Adventist, who asked him the routine question, "What's the news, Captain Bates?"

Bates replied, "The news is that the seventh day is the Sabbath of the Lord our God." Hall and Bates kept the next Sabbath. Bates wrote a book about the Sabbath and traveled as far as Michigan to preach about it.

Let's follow in the footsteps of the pioneers and repeat together the fourth commandment.

FOURTH COMMANDMENT

Time Machine Button 4

The year: 1848. The place: Dorchester, Massachusetts. During a meeting at the home of Otis Nichols, Ellen White had a vision. She said afterward to her husband, "I have a message for you. You must begin to print a little paper and send it out to the people."

After a pause she said, "From this small beginning it was shown to me to be like streams of light that went clear round the world." It was an impressive prophecy to present to a handful of poverty-stricken pioneers.

First James White published *Present Truth*. Then he began one called *Advent Review*. Its purpose was to review the evidence that the Advent movement of 1844 was truly of God. It was intended to help the believers never forget the way the Lord had led them. This was the beginning of the *Adventist Review*, our church paper.

Right now would be a good time to review why we are Seventh-day Adventists. Why did you join the church? What evidence do you have that it is the true church?

We'll take a couple of minutes to share why we are Adventists. Let's reaffirm our faith to one another. Find someone who is not your spouse. Get into groups of two or three and share. You'll have two minutes for sharing.

SMALL GROUP SHARING

Time Machine Button 5

The time: 1874. The place: Battle Creek, Michigan. On August 14, 1874, the General Conference Committee voted the following historic action: "Resolved, that the General Conference instruct the executive committee to send Elder J. N. Andrews to Switzerland as soon as practicable." He sailed from Boston on September 15, 1874.

From that humble beginning has grown a mission program that circles the globe. Today our report is from _____.

MISSION REPORT

Time Machine Button 6

The Year: 1890. The Place: Oakland, California. The missionary sailing ship, *Pitcairn*, sailed for the South Sea Islands with six missionaries on board. It had been built by funds raised by North American Sabbath schools.

Every family had a mission savings bank in which to put pennies and dimes to help build *Pitcairn*.

Today giving to missions is a part of every Sabbath school program. We still have a tremendous task to take the message to more than 1,600 people groups that have absolutely no Christian witness. More than 2.5 billion people have never heard the gospel message. Please give generously when the offering envelope is passed around today.

Time Machine Button 7

The time: 1852. The place: Rochester, New York. The first number of *Youth's Instructor* was published in Rochester, New York. In it were the first Sabbath school lessons.

Elder James White wrote many of the first lessons while traveling to speaking appointments in New England. He would often write using his lunch box or the top of his hat for a desk while he rested under a tree with his horse grazing nearby.

We will now divide for lesson study.

LESSON STUDY

Discover Your Spiritual Gifts

12

Preparation

Make copies of the Spiritual Gifts Survey for each member of your Sabbath school. Have pencils ready for those who need them.

Prepare caring certificates.

Buy seven small gifts to illustrate the seven clusters of spiritual gifts. Suggested gifts are: calendar, pocket concordance, praying hands plaque, world bank, cup or mug, booklet on tongues or healing, notepad. You may think of other appropriate items that could remind people of a particular group of spiritual gifts.

Gift wrap each item, using large boxes for a greater effect. Inside each box will be the gift and a set of instructions to read. Arrange the gifts on a table. Do not number the gifts.

This is a surprise audience participation program. The order in which the parcels are opened does not make any difference. Ask for volunteers to open the parcels. Have someone appointed ahead of time to give the mission report.

Opening Remarks

Good morning! I'm glad you're on time this morning because we have some gifts for you! No, they are not for your birthday, and it's a long time until Christmas! Today we'll unwrap these presents and discover your spiritual gifts, those special gifts that the Holy Spirit has given to help the church grow and prosper.

Inside these presents you'll find gifts of leadership, gifts of thinking, gifts of devotion, gifts of sharing, gifts of caring, gifts of communication, and gifts of verification. And although there are only seven parcels, there are 22 gifts inside these seven parcels.

In fact, our whole Sabbath school program is centered around opening these packages and discovering the 22 gifts of the Spirit. Since the gifts are for you, I'm going to ask seven of you to volunteer to open the parcels. There is actually a gift inside the package that you can keep. It is something that will remind us of a cluster of spiritual gifts.

All you have to do is come up here, select a gift, open it, and read whatever is on the card that goes with the gift. When you are finished you may keep the gift.

As we discover the spiritual gifts inside each parcel, I want you to try to discover your own spiritual gifts. *(Distribute Spiritual Gifts Survey.)* You are now receiving a Spiritual Gifts Survey. As each parcel is opened, there will be a description of the three or four spiritual gifts in one of the categories. Your job is to decide whether or not you have that gift. Check the gifts you think you have. Place a question mark if you are not sure. You may be surprised at the number of gifts that you have!

OK! Let's begin! I want to see what is in these presents, don't you? Who will help us discover our gifts? Come on! This is going to be exciting! The packages are not numbered, so you may take whichever one you choose.

Gifts of Leadership—Package 1 (Calendar)

A calendar is a tool leaders use to organize their work for the Lord. The three gifts of leadership are administration, apostleship, and shepherding.

Administration is the ability to organize and manage, working with and through others to achieve goals. Is that your gift? Please mark it on your Spiritual Gifts Survey if it is.

Apostleship in 199- is the Spirit-given ability to begin new work and establish new churches. Do you have this gift? If so, check it on the survey.

Shepherding or *pastoring* is the capacity to guide, feed, and protect a group of believers in Christ. If you sense that you have this gift, check it on the survey.

DISCOVER YOUR SPIRITUAL GIFTS

The Adventist Church has grown to what it is because of the men and women who possessed the gifts of administration, apostleship, and shepherding. Let's see if you can name a few of these individuals.

1. The third president of the General Conference helped establish several new churches in Europe. Who was he? *(J. N. Andrews)*
2. Along with D. T. Bourdeau this man opened up the work on the Pacific Coast and was later sent to develop new work in England. His name was _____. *(J. N. Loughborough)*
3. This former Methodist minister used his gifts to inaugurate the first Adventist school at Bucks Bridge, New York. He was also the first General Conference president. *(John Byington)*
4. He began the work in Battle Creek as well as in many other towns from New England to Michigan. He chaired the 1860 organizational meeting. He was _____. *(Joseph Bates)*
5. This gifted woman directed the work of the Sabbath school for 21 years. *(L. Flora Plummer)*

Gifts of Thinking—Package 2 (Pocket Concordance)
This pocket concordance reminds us of the three gifts of thinking: knowledge, discernment, and wisdom.

Knowledge is the ability to store and recall a fund of facts and other details from Scripture. Those who know their Bibles and can quote texts for what they believe have this gift. Do you have this ability? If so, please mark it on your survey.

Discernment is the ability to distinguish between truth and error, right and wrong. Check this talent on your Spiritual Gifts Survey if you have this particular gift.

Wisdom is the ability to penetrate into a matter, seeing the situation in its larger relationships and imparting wise counsel from God's Word. Wisdom is a gift that God wants to give to all of us. James 1:5 says that all we need to do is ask for wisdom and He will give it to us. Let's ask Him for that gift now, as we kneel for prayer.

PRAYER

Gifts of Devotion—Package 3 (Prayer Plaque)

Faith, intercessory prayer, and martyrdom are the three gifts of devotion.

Faith is the unusual ability to recognize in a given situation that which God intends to do and to trust Him for it until He brings it to pass. If God has blessed you with faith, please put a check mark near this item on your Spiritual Gifts Survey.

Intercessory prayer is the ability to intercede on behalf of another person through faith in the promises of God. Do you have this ability? Then put a check by it.

Martyrdom is that special ability given to some people who are required to suffer for the faith even to death—all the while consistently showing a joyous victorious attitude.

Let's sing about this faith of our fathers that kept them true in difficult times.

CONGREGATIONAL SONG: "Faith of Our Fathers," No. 304, in *The SDA Hymnal.*

Gifts of Sharing—Package 4 (World Globe Bank)

This globe reminds us of the three gifts for sharing the good news of the gospel with the whole world: missionary, evangelism, and giving.

A *missionary* is anyone with the ability to minister across cultural boundaries. If God's Spirit has bestowed this gift on you, please put a check mark by it on your survey.

Evangelism is the ability to persuasively present the gospel so that people are led to become Christians. Check this gift if you have it.

Giving is the capacity to share liberally to meet the needs of others and yet to do so with a purity of motive which senses that giving is a simple sharing of what God has provided. Do you have this gift?

Our mission reports tell us about the work of missionaries and evangelists around the world. The purpose of these reports is to show us how we can use the gift of giving to help take the message of Christ's soon return to every nation, kindred, and tribe on Planet Earth.

Today _____ will tell us about using the sharing gifts in _____.

MISSION REPORT

Gifts of Caring—Package 5 (Cup or Mug)

To offer someone a drink is to say "I care about you!" The gifts of caring include mercy, hospitality, and service.

Mercy is the capacity to feel sympathy for those in need and to manifest this sympathy in some practical way with a cheerful spirit so as to encourage and help the one who is suffering. Might you have this ability? If so, please mark it.

Hospitality is the capacity to provide an open house and graciousness to those in need of food, lodging, and fellowship so that guests are refreshed physically and spiritually. Is this an ability God has given you?

Service is the ability to unselfishly meet the needs of others through some type of practical help. The exercise of this gift often releases someone with a teaching or preaching gift to pursue his or her outreach. Cleaning the church, fixing a roof, or giving someone a ride are examples of this gift in action. Is this your gift?

We have many people in our church who have the gifts of caring. Now I'm going to ask you to help me award some Caring Certificates.

CARING CERTIFICATES *(Certificates of award or achievement are available through Christian bookstores or teachers' supply stores. Secure 10 of these. Fill in everything except the name. Award the certificates to those with achievements in caring.)* Today we have 10 caring awards to present. The certificates say that these people are being honored for their achievement in caring.

There are no names on these certificates. You get to nominate these 10 individuals. All you need to do is come to the front and say the name of one person who deserves an award because of his or her caring. You must also tell why you think this person deserves the award. Give a specific example of one of his or her caring acts. I will fill in the name, and you will present the certificate to the individual.

There are two rules we must follow. No person may receive more than one certificate. And the person nominated must be present here in the sanctuary this morning.

Gifts of Communication—Package 6 (Notepad)

A notepad could help you use your gifts of communication: teaching, prophecy, and exhortation.

Teaching is the ability to explain Bible truths in such a way that those willing to learn will understand. Are you good at explaining things to others? Then please put a check mark by this gift listed on your Spiritual Gifts Survey.

Prophecy refers primarily to the gift of one who is called to receive divine revelation from God. It can also refer to the capacity to preach so that the Bible comes alive to hearers. Can you do that?

Exhortation is also sometimes called the gift of encouragement. It is the capacity to urge people to action in terms of applying Scripture truth or to encourage and comfort people by applying Bible truths to their needs. If Jesus has enabled you to do this, don't forget to mark this gift on the survey.

Let's use the gift of encouragement right now. Everyone stand up. Find someone who is not your spouse and share a Bible text that could be of help to this person in his or her Christian walk. You'll have two minutes for this exercise.

SMALL GROUP SHARING

Gifts of Verification—Package 7 (Booklet on Healing or Tongues)

Tongues, interpretation of tongues, miracles, and healing are often called the "signs" gifts. They are given to authenticate a work as being from God.

DISCOVER YOUR SPIRITUAL GIFTS

Tongues is an ability given by the Holy Spirit to an individual to speak spontaneously in a foreign language unknown to the speaker.

Interpretation is a special ability given by the Holy Spirit to translate spontaneously the statements of someone with the gift of tongues.

Miracles is the special ability that God gives certain people to perform acts which alter the ordinary course of nature.

Healing is that special ability which God gives to certain people through whom He cures illness and restores health.

In the Bible one of the chapters that deals with spiritual gifts is 1 Corinthians 12. You'll find this as responsive reading No. 776 in *The SDA Hymnal. (Lead the audience in this responsive reading.)*

RESPONSIVE READING

SPIRITUAL GIFTS SURVEY

Gifts of Leadership
____ Administration ____ Apostleship ____ Shepherding

Gifts of Thinking
____ Discernment ____ Wisdom ____ Knowledge

Gifts of Devotion
____ Faith ____ Intercession ____ Martyrdom

Gifts of Sharing
____ Missionary ____ Evangelism ____ Giving

Gifts of Caring

____ Mercy ____ Hospitality ____ Service

Gifts of Communication
____ Teaching ____ Prophecy ____ Exhortation

Gifts of Verification
____ Tongues ____ Miracles ____ Interpretation
____ Healing

Travelogue

Euro-Africa Holiday

———— 13 ————

Preparation

Suggest that your song leader choose songs originating from countries in the Euro-Africa Division. Here is a sample list from *The SDA Hymnal:* Italian, Nos. 370, 71; Austrian, No. 423; Spanish, No. 295; German, Nos. 506, 559, 383, 240, 91; French, Nos. 28, 115.

(Duplicate copies of "¡Cristo Muy Pronto Vendra!" and the Missions Quiz for everyone present.)

Program

(Have telephone on pulpit. Lift the receiver and speak as though answering the phone.)

/ Hello! _____ speaking from the _____ SDA Church. ¿Quien habla? . . . Allo! . . . Na'am . . . Pronto! . . . ¿Esta la? . . . Hallo! . . . ¡Si! ¡Si! . . . Ja! . . . Oui! . . . ¡Gracias! . . . Merci! . . . Danke schon! . . . ¡Adios! . . . Adieu! . . . Auf Wiedersehen! *(Hang up.)*

This morning I bring you greetings from the Euro-Africa Division. I spoke in Portuguese, Arabic, Italian, Spanish, French, and German. I gave the typical telephone greeting, the words "yes," "thank you," and "goodbye."

On a Euro-Africa holiday we would encounter all these languages as well as Czechoslovakian, Romanian, Bulgarian, Bantu, and a number of other African languages and dialects. This morning we take you on a 30-minute tour of the Euro-Africa Division.

Germany

We'll begin our tour in Germany at the Friedensau Theological

Graduate School. Sabbath school is just beginning, and they are singing Martin Luther's famous hymn "Ein' Feste Burg"—"A Mighty Fortress Is Our God." *(Or choose another hymn of German origin.)* Let's join them in singing No. 506 in *The SDA Hymnal.*

OPENING SONG

France

Now we must hurry to the Institut Adventiste du Saleve in France. We pause at the door while we hear a brother praying in French. We recognize the Lord's Prayer. *(If you have no one who can speak French, then have someone read the following prayer.)*

Notre Père qui es dans les cieux, que ton Nom soit sanctifié, que ton Règne arrive, que ta Volonté soit faite sur la terre comme au ciel. Donne-nous aujourd'hui notre pain quotidien. Remets-nous nos dettes comme nous-même avons remis à no débiteurs. Et ne nous soumets à la tentation, mais délivre-nous du Mauvais. Car à toi appartiennent le royaume et la puissance et la gloire pour les siècles. Amen!

(Alternative: Have everyone repeat the Lord's Prayer in the language they feel most comfortable with.)

LORD'S PRAYER

Our brothers and sisters in Europe and Africa love John 3:16 just as much as we do. Is there anyone here who can recite John 3:16 in one of the following languages: Portuguese, Spanish, French, German, Italian, Czechoslovakian, Romanian, Bulgarian, Arabic, or Bantu? I'm asking for volunteers. *(You might be surprised who of your members can do this. If you know people from these nationalities, contact them ahead of time to be prepared to recite this verse. If you know people of these nationalities who are not Adventists, invite them to come and recite it for your program. Most cities will have people who speak these languages, and the effect is worth the trouble of finding them.)*

TRANSLATION OF LOVE: John 3:16

Spain

SPECIAL MUSIC: "Lift Up the Trumpet" in Spanish. *(Ask one of the children's divisions to learn this song, or have a group of Spanish people sing it. Duplicate copies for the audience. Have them join in at the italicized parts.)*
¡CRISTO MUY PRONTO VENDRA!
1. Sier-vos de Dios in trom-pe-ta to-cad;
    ¡Cris-to muy pron-to ven-dra!
A to-do el mun-do el men-sa-je lle-vad;
¡Cris-to muy pron-to ven-dra!

Chorus: *¡Pron-to ven-dra! ¡Pron-to ven-dra!*
    ¡Cris-to muy pron-to ven-dra!

2. Fie-les de Cris-to, de pri-sa a -nun-ciad;
¡Cris-to muy pron-to ven-dra!
Gra-tos, a-le-gres, con-ten-tos, can-tad,
¡Cris-to muy pron-to ven-dra!

3. Mon-tes y va-lles, el son re-so-nad;
¡Cris-to muy pron-to ven-dra!
On-das del mar la can-cion en-to-nad,
¡Cris-to muy pron-to ven-dra!

4. Gue-rras y ham-bres nos dan a en-ten-der;
¡Cris-to muy pron-to ven-dra!
Tiem-bla la tie-rra y nos ha-ce sa-ber;
¡Cris-to muy pron-to ven-dra!
—James Strout, in *Melodias de Victoria* (Pacific Press Pub. Assn.)

Austria

Our last stop is Seminar Schloss Bogenhofen in Austria, where we are just in time for a quiz on the Euro-Africa Division. You'll find these quiz sheets in your bulletin. *(Or have the ushers distribute them now.)* As the young people ask the questions, mark your choice. They will then give you the correct answers, and you can see how much you know. *(Choose 8 juniors, earliteens, or youth to present these questions and answers.)*

MISSION QUIZ

1. The country of the Euro-Africa Division with the largest number of churches is: (a) Germany (b) Angola (c) Mozambique (d) Romania.

2. The country with the fewest Adventist churches is (a) Algeria (b) Austria (c) Spain (d) Switzerland.

3. The country with the most baptized Adventist believers is (a) Germany (b) Mozambique (c) Angola (d) Romania.

4. In which of the following countries is the Portuguese language *not* of major importance? (a) Portugal (b) Algeria (c) Angola (d) Mozambique.

5. Seventh-day Adventist beliefs were first preached in Italy, Switzerland, and Romania by (a) D. T. Bourdeau (b) L. R. Conradi (c) J. N. Andrews (d) M. B. Czechowski.

6. J. N. Andrews first heard from a beggar of Sabbathkeeping Adventists in (a) Germany (b) Austria (c) Italy (d) France.

7. Joseph Gomis, while on a trip to Switzerland, learned of the Seventh-day Adventists through *Signs of the Times*. He returned to his country, set up a bakery, and witnessed to his family and friends. This was the beginning of Adventist work in (a) Algeria (b) Romania (c) Spain (d) Portugal.

8. In six of the following countries the Roman Catholic Church is not the main denomination. Check those six countries. ____ Portugal, ____ Czechoslovakia, ____ Switzerland, ____ Spain,

___ Belgium, ___ Angola, ___ France, ___ Germany, ___ Romania, ___ Italy, ___ Austria, ___ Bulgaria, ___ Algeria, ___ Mozambique.

ANSWERS

1. The correct answer is *Romania*. Germany has 601 churches. Angola has 552. Mozambique has 637. But Romania has 923.

2. You should have circled *Algeria*. There we have only two congregations. Austria has 44; Spain, 56; and Switzerland, 56.

3. The correct answer is *Angola*. We have 141,374 brothers and sisters in Angola. Germany has 34,365; Mozambique, 86,836; and Romania is in third place with 67,445 members.

4. You should have circled *Algeria*. It was once a French colony. Both Angola and Mozambique were Portuguese.

5. You should have circled *M. B. Czechowski*. Czechowski, a former Polish Catholic priest, joined the Adventist Church in Findlay, Ohio, in 1857. He wanted to go as a missionary to Italy, but the young Adventist Church was not ready to send him. He therefore got assistance from another Adventist denomination, which sent him to Europe in 1864. He formed a company in Torre Pellice in a Waldensian valley in Italy and taught them SDA doctrines. Later he preached the Adventist message in Switzerland and Romania.

D. T. Bourdeau was a French-speaking evangelist from Canada and was sent to help J. N. Andrews. L. R. Conradi was a German-speaking missionary who worked in central Europe, Eastern Europe, and Russia. J. N. Andrews was the first SDA foreign missionary in Europe.

6. The answer is *Germany*. Sometime in the mid-nineteenth century J. H. Lindermann, a weaver by trade, concluded from his study that Jesus would come soon. In 1867 he found the Sabbath truth from his personal study. He published his views and organized several groups that followed his teachings.

News of these Sabbathkeeping followers of Lindermann was carried to Swiss Adventists by a wandering beggar. As a result, James Erzberger, the first ordained SDA minister in Europe, visited them and baptized the first SDAs in Germany.

7. The correct answer is *Algeria.*

8. You should have checked *Germany* and *Switzerland,* which are mainly Protestant countries; Romania is Greek Orthodox; in Algeria and Bulgaria Islam is the major religion; and in Mozambique the majority of the people are animists.

Our final stop is _____ to hear a mission report by _____.

MISSION REPORT

Variety Program

The Starless Crown

Preparation

The Sabbath school council should meet and decide on a soul-winning project, such as a missing members campaign. Compile a list of names. Divide the names among the classes and enlist the teachers to put into action a program of contacting these missing members. Phone calls, personal visits, greeting cards, and an invitation to a potluck are some of the avenues that could be used.

Program

Talk 1: "Rescue on the Lake"

One morning in Evanston, Illinois, word came that a steamer was in distress on the lake. The life-saving crew hurried to the shore. There they saw the *Lady Elgin* crumbling under the power of the storm. Men and women were in danger of being lost.

Among the life-saving crew were two brothers from Iowa. One of these stripped off all surplus clothing and swam out and brought one passenger to the shore. He went again and brought another, and then another, and another, until there were nine on the shore of Lake Michigan. He was chilled to the bone.

As he stood there trembling before the fire, he saw another man in peril and said, "I must go again."

The crowd gathered around him, saying, "It doesn't mean rescue for him if you go. It means death for you." But he broke from the crowd and plunged into the icy waters and brought a tenth, and an eleventh, and a twelfth to the shore.

Again he stood by the fire, his strength apparently all gone. As they looked at him there, so blue and chilled with cold, it seemed as if death had put its hand upon him. But he looked again toward the wreck and saw others in danger. Once more he struck out through the storm and brought a thirteenth, a fourteenth, and a fifteenth to shore.

Cold and exhausted, he stood once more by the fire. But he could not rest. The victims of the storm lay upon his heart.

Once more he looked out and saw a beam drifting toward the shore. Clinging to that beam was a man and his wife. The beam was drifting around a point of land that meant death to those in peril. Weak as he was, the young man from Iowa plunged again into the water, grasped the beam, and with his remaining strength swung it around the perilous point and brought both the husband and his wife to land.

That afternoon as the young man—pale and exhausted—stood in his room with his roommate, he said, "Did I do my best? Did I do my very best? Oh, I am afraid I did not do my very best!"

As the young hero tossed in delirium that night, his brother sat beside him and tried to comfort him by telling him, "You saved 17!"

"Oh," replied the young man, "if only I could have saved one more!"

This thrilling incident expresses the object of our Sabbath school—the saving of souls for eternity.

Have you done your best for Jesus? Have you done your very best? How many lost persons have you helped find Him? How many chained persons have you helped free?

SPECIAL MUSIC: "Have I Done My Best for Jesus?"

Talk 2: "Soul Winning by Caring"
All about us people are perishing, "having no hope and without God in the world." Even within our own church are those who have never yielded their lives to Christ.

What a vast field of neglected opportunities faces most of us! We claim to be Christians. We go through the ritual of Sabbath school every week, but many of us have never ventured to make personal heart-to-heart appeals to those who have not been born again. If Christ should come today, the vast majority of us would stand before the throne condemned, ashamed for our neglected opportunities for witnessing.

How often we have sung "Will There Be Any Stars in My Crown?" And strange as it may seem, we are quite content to let the question rest with no answer. The melody dies away, and eternity's crown fades into oblivion.

In *Testimonies*, volume 5, we are told that the "angels are employed in making crowns" (p. 96) for the redeemed and that the "crowns of the saints are of most pure gold, decked with stars" and that the stars represent souls won for Christ (*Early Writings*, p. 54).

We are assured that there is a crown for every saint and that Jesus "with His own right hand" will place these crowns on our heads (*ibid.*, p. 16). The scene as viewed by the servant of God is very vivid. She saw some of the saints with very bright crowns, others not so bright. Some crowns appeared heavy with stars, while others had but a few. And we are urged to aim in the strength of Jesus for the crown heavy with stars.

Will there by any stars in *your* crown? Have you spoken to your children about salvation? Are there missing members in your Sabbath school class whom you could win back through love? Do you have a neighbor who needs to hear the invitation of Jesus?

Don't you see? People are in peril. Multitudes are perishing. But what do we care? Who of us is burdened for these souls? While the destiny of a world hangs in the balance, we simply shrug our shoulders and make excuses.

Hidden Mike: "There is a stupor, a paralysis upon the people of God, which prevents them from understanding the duty of the hour. . . . The professed followers of Christ are on trial before the heavenly universe; but the coldness of their zeal and the feebleness of their efforts in God's service mark them as unfaithful" (*Christ's Object Lessons*, p. 303).

Let's change the picture by our earnest efforts during the next few weeks. If we are faithful, there will surely be some stars in our crowns!

Poem: "The Starless Crown"

"Wearied and worn with earthly care, I yielded to repose,
And soon before my raptured sight a glorious vision rose.
I thought, while slumbering on my couch in midnight's
	awful gloom,
I heard an angel's silvery voice, and radiance filled my
	room.
A gentle touch awakened me, a gentle whisper said,
'Arise, O sleeper, follow me!' and through the air we fled.
We left the earth so far away that like a speck it seemed,
And heavenly glory, calm and pure, across our pathway
	streamed.
Still on we went; my soul was rapt in silent ecstasy;
I wondered what the end would be, what next would meet
	my eye.
I knew not how we journeyed through the pathless fields of
	light,
When suddenly a change was wrought, and I was clothed
	in white.
We stood before a city's walls, most glorious to behold;
We passed through gates of glittering pearl, o'er streets of
	purest gold.
It needed not the sun by day, nor silver moon by night;
The glory of the Lord was there, the Lamb Himself its
	light.
Bright angels paced the shining street, sweet music filled
	the air,
And white-robed saints, with glittering crowns, from every
	clime were there.
And some that I had loved on earth stood with them round
	the throne;
"All worthy is the Lamb," they sang, "the glory His
	alone!"
But fairer far than all beside, I saw my Saviour's face,
And as I gazed, He smiled on me with wondrous love and

grace.

Slowly I bowed before His throne, o'erjoyed that I at last
Had gained the object of my hopes, that earth at length was
    past.
And then in solemn tones He said, 'Where is the diadem
That ought to sparkle on thy brow, adorned with many a
    gem?
I know thou hast believed on me, and life, through Me, is
    thine,
But where are all those radiant stars that in thy crown
    should shine?
Yonder thou seest a glorious throng, and stars on every
    brow!
For every soul they led to Me, they wear a jewel now!
And such thy bright reward had been if such had been thy
    deed,
If thou hadst sought some wandering feet in paths of peace
    to lead;
I did not mean that thou shouldst tread the way of life
    alone,
But that the clear and shining light which round thy foot-
    steps shone
Should guide some other weary feet to My bright home of
    rest,
And thus in blessing those around, thou hadst thyself been
    blest.'
The vision faded from my sight; the voice no longer spake;
A spell seemed brooding o'er my soul, which long I feared
    to break;
And when at last I gazed around, in morning's glimmering
    light,
My spirit felt o'erwhelmed beneath that vision's awful
    night.
I rose and wept with chastened joy that yet I dwelt below,
That yet another hour was mine, my faith by works to
    show,

That yet some sinner I might tell of Jesus' dying love,
And help to lead some weary soul to seek a home above.
And now while on the earth I stay, my motto this shall be,
'To live no longer to myself, but Him who died for me.'
And graven on my inmost soul this word of truth divine,
'They that turn many to the Lord bright as the stars shall
    shine.' "

—*Author Unknown*

from G. B. Thompson, *Soul Winning* (Review and Herald Pub. Assn., 1916), pp. 190-192.

CONGREGATIONAL SONG: "I Am Thinking Today of That Beautiful Land," *The Church Hymnal*, No. 626.

Superintendent: One of the ways we have of winning souls is through giving our mission offerings. Without our systematic giving week by week, our mission program would have to be drastically reduced. Through our sacrificial giving, God is calling out a firmament of chosen ones who someday will be in the kingdom. Today our mission report tells about souls won through your giving.

MISSION REPORT

Also by Dorothy Eaton Watts

Three more planners for busy Sabbath school leaders

Sabbath School Program Planner, book 1
Book 1 provides 12 dynamic programs complete with scripts.
You'll find suggestions for scripture, responsive reading, special
music, and song service. Plus 65 fresh ideas for creating your
own exciting programs. Paper, 96 pages. US$7.95, Cdn$11.55.

Sabbath School Program Planner, book 2
Book 2 gives you 14 complete programs with entire scripts for
holidays and special occasions. Many include suggestions for
prayer, responsive readings, special music, and congregational
songs. Paper, 107 pages. US$7.95, Cdn$11.55.

Sabbath School Program Planner, book 3
The ingenious Dorothy Eaton Watts returns with 14 creative and
complete programs for Sabbath school leaders. She also gives
you 14 summertime strategies that can keep programs interesting
and spiritually rewarding in spite of lower attendance. Paper, 112
pages. US$7.95, Cdn$11.55.
